Time to Pivot

Shifting from Ideation to Execution to Sustainability

TYRA SELDON, Ph.D.

Copyright© 2019 by Tyra Seldon, Ph.D.
All Rights Reserved
First Edition

ISBN: 9781799141660

No part of this publication may be reproduced or transmitted in any form or by any electronic or mechanical means, including informational storage and retrieval systems, except by a reviewer who may quote brief passages in a review.

Printed in the United States of America

This book is lovingly dedicated to my late father, Clarence E. Seldon, who introduced me to the love of language and the craft of writing.

TABLE OF CONTENTS

IDEATION

What is Your Idea? 1

The Value of Making Mistakes..21

Investing in Yourself..34

Techniques for Developing Your Idea..60

EXECUTION

Leveraging Your Credentials, Prior Knowledge and Life Experiences...78

Branding Yourself: By Design or By Default?...88

Business or Expensive Hobby?..100

SUSTAINABILITY

Money Matters: Are You Prepared to be the Boss?............................123

Making Sustainability A Cornerstone of Your Business......................152

Tyra L. Seldon, Ph.D.

INTRODUCTION

TIRED OF BEING A CAGED BIRD

I know why the caged bird sings.

-Paul Laurence Dunbar

$20,000.00. It is an amount that I will never forget and it is the amount that cemented my desire to find fair and equitable ways to share my gifts with others. I was a new hire at an institution and a casual lunch conversation revealed that one of my male colleagues was making exactly $20,000 more than I was. He had fewer years of teaching experience than I did and our education levels were drastically different. It was not the first, nor the last time, that I would encounter unequal pay for equal, or more, work. In many ways, I felt like a caged bird. I could see through the bars, but I was not free.

If you are aware of Horatio Alger's "Ragged Dick" story then you're probably familiar with the rags to riches motif that has captured readers' imaginations for over a century. At the core of that story is the idea that regardless of race, gender, or socio-economic class, we all have the same opportunities to achieve our professional and personal goals. Many of us seek out professions and jobs that will allow us to ascend to the top. Interestingly, even when I worked at the most progressive of institutions, I never experienced that type of parity. Yet, I stayed and I waited and I waited (which I will discuss in greater detail in Chapter 1).

Although I was uncomfortable, I was comfortable. There were times when I should have moved and I did not and times when I moved, when I should have stayed in place. In many ways, my entire life has revolved around pivoting, or movement. The problem is that I was moving, but not with great intentionality or purpose, so it felt more like meandering. And I know I am not alone.

On the surface, this may seem to be over the top or hinged on paranoia, but the reality of not being compensated or treated fairly is real. I often hear my friends, many of whom have climbed the proverbial corporate and academic ladders, complain about being mistreated, overworked, and frustrated by some of their experiences with overt and blatant forms of discrimination. Although no 'job' is perfect, entrepreneurship often offers a different trajectory—one that can give us a glimpse of what it feels like to be in a space where one's productivity and creativity is not controlled or dominated by someone else.

In fact, at various points in my life, typically after I applied for a position, I could always tell when potential employers were checking me out. My email would sprout up with numerous reminders that, "Tyra, people are looking at your LinkedIn profile."

Ugh!

For me, launching a business was the most liberating thing that I have ever done and I hope that as you embark on this journey with me in *Time to Pivot,* you too will think about whether or not it is time for you to pivot.

Why now?

I write for various national outlets and platforms. Every day, I get inbox messages and emails from readers, especially women. In my mind, I call it 'Tyra Mail' (thank you, Tyra Banks for the idea). Although readers of all backgrounds will find value in this book, I want to especially encourage women who feel marginalized in the entrepreneurial ecosystem or who have yet to find mentors to help them navigate this nuanced and complicated space.

Many of us, by default or by choice, are caregivers. We find ourselves being the CEOs of other people's lives. This often requires learning how to integrate our needs with the needs of others. Whether it is shuffling children to and from co-curricular activities or supporting elderly parents, it is difficult for many women to carve out time for themselves. It is also difficult to ask for help.

We confuse the idea of a democracy with that of a meritocracy. So if something isn't working out or it has failed, it must be our fault, right? Wrong! Meritocracy is built on the idea that we are rewarded based upon our achievement, or the merit of our work, including our intellect. In some industries and fields, meritocracy is just an ideal.

To a certain extent, the changes that we see unfolding before our eyes with e-commerce, digitization, and open resources is changing how we all do business; it is also creating a more level playing field.

For example, in my industry as a professional writer, a good article or blog, whether written by a male author or a female author, can still fetch the same rate of compensation. Competitive pricing and quality work are privileged and not someone's gender or race. I have rarely, if ever, wondered if someone was getting paid more simply because he was born a male or with a different hue of skin.

Depending on what you do, you may never meet or even see your clients. E-commerce has made entrepreneurship fertile ground for a meritocracy where one's zip code, last name, or gender doesn't translate into grounds for preferential treatment or, conversely, discrimination. Acquiring new projects, building clientele and receiving referrals is often based upon the quality of one's work.

Of course, entrepreneurship is not utopic; however, it is a space where one's creativity, intellect, skill sets, and gifts seem to be respected for their intrinsic and extrinsic value which is why I decided to write this book.

Do we really need another book about entrepreneurship?

Great question. My answer is yes! If economists are correct, our world is changing. Many of us who imagined working for corporations, universities and even the government may find ourselves forging into an area that we never imagined and if you are like me, it may lead you to entrepreneurship—a path that you may not have envisioned for yourself.

And that is why I wrote this book: It is my honest attempt to share with you a journey that propelled me from employee to freelancer to entrepreneur and now, employer. It is not filled with clichés and a laundry list of 'if you do this, I guarantee this will happen'. It is also not filled with business jargon. There is no MBA behind my name; in fact, as I will discuss later in the book, all of my degrees are in English and I have never taken a business class.

Yet, in 2011, at the prompting of my spirit, I took a leap of faith and left behind an industry that I loved—academia—to pursue professional writing as a vocation. Throughout this journey, I have made some mistakes; I have been humbled; I have experienced great sacrifice; however; I have gained wisdom; I have gained insight; and yes, I have gained a tenacity and determination that Seldon Writing Group, LLC will leave a positive imprint in this world.

So, yes, this book is about motivating you. But I don't just want you to feel motivated and inspired; I want you to take action—to revisit your dreams and to execute and sustain them. *Time to Pivot* is an honest look at a journey that was much like Odysseus' travels in Homer's *The Odyssey*. From figuring out how to register my LLC to understanding the nuances of a 1099 status and attracting high value clients, *Time to Pivot* is filled with some practical steps that you can implement as well as some pitfalls to avoid as you pivot.

In the spirit of transparency, there is not a clear, universal path to entrepreneurship, but in the process of figuring it out (which is an ongoing process), I learned a few things that I'd like to share with you and rather than just writing one long continuous prose book, I wrote this as a series of intertwining and interconnected vignettes that address key aspects of how you can shift from ideation to execution to sustainability.

As such the book is organized in three stages of business development: ideation, execution, and sustainability. To shift from one of these to the next, it requires movement. Unfortunately, it is during the first two stages that many of us give up. I hope that the information presented here will help you shift.

Whereas writing is the gift that served as my springboard for my journey, yours may be photography, public speaking, graphic design, accounting, event planning, legal counsel, non-profit work, ministry, or some variation thereof. I have crafted this book in such a way that you will be able to see yourself as a part of the larger, unfolding narrative. Written in non-sequential order, *Time to Pivot's* chapters are arranged topically with the intent of educating, empowering, and encouraging readers.

Chapter Organization and Synopsis

Ideation Chapters

Chapter One: What is Your Idea?

This chapter explores the concept of understanding and unpacking your idea. Ideas may come in the form of dreams, visions, conversations, a problem that needs to be solved or innovation. No matter where it comes from, the key is do you know what to do with it?

Chapter Two: The Value of Making Mistakes

There is this misnomer that perfection or getting things right are the only ways to grow or get better. I'd like to disrupt that mode of thinking by suggesting that our mistakes, our failures, and yes, our mess-ups actually make us better at our craft.

Chapter Three: Investing in Yourself

The thought of going back to high school or a college campus as an adult may be daunting; therefore, self-study is often not only more appealing, but more practical for most people. However, it is not the only way to invest in yourself. As with most things, time on task is critical. If you are serious about investing in yourself, then be prepared to do the work that it requires.

Chapter Four: Techniques for Developing your Idea
When most ideas present themselves, they are not perfect. In fact,

many ideas will undergo numerous reiterations before they are cemented as the 'right one.' The key is to not give up or abandon the concept. When you discover strategies and techniques for improving your idea, you are more likely to execute it.

Execution Chapters

<u>Chapter Five: Leveraging your Credentials, Prior Knowledge and Life Experiences</u>

Whether a new or established business owner, many of us underestimate the fact that new ideas are constantly oscillating around them. Too often we may think that we are too old, or too young, to fully execute an idea—not true! Some of the most successful people were able to become leaders because they knew how to leverage their knowledge, credentials, and prior knowledge to move forward—do you?

<u>Chapter Six: Branding Yourself: By Design or By Default</u>

In order to monetize, it is important that you understand the business side of being an entrepreneur. Most successful business owners spend time branding themselves, building up their network, and building a sustainable fan-base. This, in turn, translates into potential sales, especially with the reach and influence of social media. This chapter will explore how you can do so without compromising who you are.

Sustainability Chapters

<u>Chapter Seven: Business or Expensive Hobby?</u>

There are those who believe that once you put a price tag on your gift, you are no longer being true to your gift; they contend that somehow the essence of the craft is diluted once you monetize it. However, history shows us that this is the furthest thing from the truth. Many individuals have successfully used their gifts as launching pads for economic success.

The key is staying true to your gift, being authentic in how you represent your gift and positioning yourself to be of service to your gift as you help other people through the manifestation of your gift—whether it is via tangible goods and/or services.

Chapter Eight: Money Matters: Are You Prepared to Be The Boss?

In this day of social media and e-commerce, everyone wants to be a boss. The term is used ubiquitously; therefore, many people don't think about what it actually means or its implications. Yet, to sustain a successful career as an entrepreneur, being a boss is something that you need to think about. In fact, how you manage money, how you organize, how you interact with other people—peers and subordinates—are often vital factors in your company's success. Although profitability is important for sustainability, so is leadership and innovation.

Whether it is just you or you hire employees or contractors, you want to give some consideration to your leadership style. What are your strengths? What are your weaknesses? Being aware of how you lead, your own belief systems, including how you deal with disappointment can be integral factors in your long-term success.

Chapter Nine: Making Sustainability as a Cornerstone of Your Business

No one wants to invest time, resources and energy into a business venture just to have it dissipate or fail shortly after starting up. The key to sustainability is often going slow and steady. In a world that is pushing you to sprint, can you endure a marathon?

With many small businesses not being able to sustain viability beyond year 3, it is important to be proactive as you think about the things that you need in your wheelhouse now in order to create longevity and future success.

Tyra L. Seldon, Ph.D.

IDEATION

1

WHAT IS YOUR IDEA?

Dreams move the wind.

-Edwidge Danticat

I grew up watching the *Star Wars* series, and as much as I wanted to gravitate towards Princes Leia like a lot of my friends, Yoda was my guy.

From his distinctive voice and interesting phenotype, I couldn't wait for him to utter his words of wisdom. And although I have several megabytes of real people who I admire and look up to, it was Yoda's advice to "train yourself to let go of everything you fear to lose" that stuck with me during my adolescent years. Little did I know that a real-life Sensei would be the driving force for a life-altering decision as an adult.

When I earned my Ph.D. in 2002, I was already teaching full time at Dickinson College in Carlisle, PA. An idyllic campus tucked away in central Pennsylvania, it was my first experience teaching full time besides my graduate assistantship at the University of Rochester.

I was blessed with some amazing colleagues in the English and American Studies departments where I had a joint appointment. My students ran the gamut from engaged, idealistic, and brilliant to apathetic and intolerant. At the time, I felt as if I could manage the responsibilities of family life, trying to teach, and launching a career.

But, something was missing. I didn't feel whole. I was good at what I did, but somehow I felt as if I were an interloper. Yet, I pushed through and kept teaching and working in the field of education. In fact, I pushed through and job hopped for several years hoping that I, like Odysseus, would eventually find my place or my way home.

In the process, I uncovered that although I was a highly skilled educator, it was not my passion. Through a series of freelancing opportunities, ghost writing, and curriculum adventures, I uncovered that my passion was writing. My gift was writing. Yet, I had no idea what to do with it.

I meandered for a few years, simply searching for the right fit and at times, I even questioned if something was wrong with me. Then I thought about my high school basketball coach, Mr. James Furcron.

Mr. Furcron, much like my father, was a no-nonsense man. He was passionate and serious about developing the young women he coached into confident basketball players and astute students. He didn't accept the words, "no" or "can't." Ironically, it wasn't about winning all of the time; it was about giving 100% all of the time. He was my real-life Yoda.

As I thought about Mr. Furcron, I remembered a concept that he wanted us to master in practice—pivoting. For some reason, pivoting seemed exceptionally difficult for me. I kept picking up both feet, which would have resulted in a travel call by the referee.

Something about moving and being still simultaneously seemed to be oxymoronic and even counterintuitive; yet, it was a skill set that I would frequently use in the game of basketball and in life.

As with any movement, pivoting requires you to assess what is around you and to move at the right time. It is also about trust. Do you trust the process that it will take to move? Have you considered the outcomes that it can lead to? For many of us, being still is easier than mastering the pivot. When both of your feet are planted firmly, you know where you stand; however, when you pivot, you are opening yourself up to change which often translates to stepping into the unknown.

Yet, if we are not open to pivoting, we risk missing out on personal and professional opportunities. In this sense, all of us, at some point, must contemplate—Is it time to pivot? For most, this leads to the follow-up question of when?

Let's Start With Childhood

Most of us learned how to dream as children. I can vividly remember reading a book and then dreaming about all of the magical places that I could visit—some were real and others were imagined. Much of my childhood and youth is anchored in books and dreams—no wonder I am so passionate about helping people write!

Although I never dreamed of being an entrepreneur, I dreamed of having the ability to help people and to create things using my imagination. Pause for a moment and think about how old you were when you were first introduced to the concept of working for yourself compared to when you actually seriously thought about doing it or did it?

Had you learned about it earlier, would it have made a difference in your career trajectory? Would you have made a pivot sooner?

The reality is that most of us, as youth, were not exposed to entrepreneurship as a viable career option unless someone in our family did it and even then, it may have been a casual association or a superficial understanding.

One of the reasons why entrepreneurship is often shrouded in a cloak of mystery is simply because many of us don't really know enough about it to understand it. In turn, the mystery continues as we become adults; yet, paradoxically most of us have experienced some form of entrepreneurship; we just didn't call it that.

Let me explain. Babysitting, tutoring, pet sitting, snow shoveling and grass cutting are just a few of the traditional ways that young people get an early taste of participating in free enterprise. [Today, young people can even use online platforms like Etsy, Shopify, and Zibbet to sell their hand made wares and crafts.]

This may seem like child's play, but think about what these types of opportunities taught us, early on, about running a sustainable business: One must have a product or service that others need; one must market and/or advertise to establish a brand; and one must offer phenomenal customer service that is aligned with the brand.

Sound familiar? So why do many of us find ourselves stuck in the ideation stage?

Ready, Set, Go

Have you ever played double Dutch? Imagine two long jump ropes moving in-sync in opposite directions at the same time. As the jump roper, you have to find the right moment to jump in without interrupting the flow of the ropes or getting your feet caught in one, or both, of the ropes.

When making the decision to start freelancing, it may feel as if you are playing a game of double Dutch—patiently waiting for the right time to *go*. If everything is not timed perfectly, you have to start all over again. In this sense, double Dutch is analogous to launching a freelancing career.

By the time most people decide to freelance, they have already figured out that they can do it and they have also figured out what they can do. Whether it is photography, writing, event planning, accounting, or graphic design, the skill typically comes before the actual freelancing. The hard part often comes with making a mental commitment to seeing it through.

Once someone has made up his/her mind to start or to go, the rest can be relatively seamless. And just like the game of double Dutch, there is a far less likely chance that you will get tripped up in the process.

So, when should you jump in?

It is Not About Numbers—There is not a set time or set age for someone to start freelancing. I started at 38 and one of my favorite clients started at 55. I know others who have started in their 20s and others who began in their teens, so starting really isn't about age; it is about preparedness.

The one thing that we all have in common is that we all felt as if we were ready; yet even that can be a nebulous concept. I knew I was ready in terms of my skill set. My older client felt as if his life experiences and credentials were his launching pad and for a 29-year-old freelancer who I mentor, her readiness was determined by having enough capital saved to leave her 9 to 5. For each of us, the motivation to push our START button was different, but none of us felt as if the decision was a premature one.

Vocation or Avocation—For some, freelancing will always maintain the position of being a source of additional income. There is nothing wrong with this. Many people enjoy freelancing on the side while also enjoying the security and fringe benefits of being someone else's employee.
But for others, the desire is so strong that just freelancing on the side or in a part time capacity is not enough. There is a tangible pull or desire to do more and to do it with greater frequency. It feels like you are purposed to do something.

Over time, especially in an American context, we seem to think of a vocation as a job, but it is more than that. Derived from the Latin word *vocationem*, your vocation is literally *a calling*. Conversely, avocation is thought of as "a calling away from one's occupation". As such, we often think of an avocation as a hobby.

I share this in order to suggest that if your desire to freelance feels more like a calling than a hobby, it just may be a sign that it is time for you to start your freelancing career. Of course, you want to make sure that you have a plan in place and that you have thought through the logistics of what you plan to do. Most importantly, make sure that starting will not create other hardships or conflicts in your life—this leads me to the third thing that you should consider.

Affordability—If there is one impediment that keeps most of us from starting, it's that we can't quite afford to freelance full time. The first time I thought about freelancing full time was as early as 2000, but I did not start until 2011. There were numerous variables at play, but one of the most important ones revolved around money. I neither had enough volume nor enough clients to make a living or enjoy the quality of life that I had grown accustomed to.

So, I waited. I kept working for other people, but **I never gave up**. Instead, I started saving and building. I saved a year's worth of my salary and paid off as much debt as I could because I planned to boot strap my business and not rely upon investors or outside funding. While others may be able to skip this step and they may opt to get funding, it is important that you try to start with capital in your reserves.

It is also important to realize that affordability isn't just about the bottom line or whether you can monetarily afford to freelance full-time. Affordability may include factoring in more than just finances; there is a need to consider how your decision affects those who you are responsible for. Not only will your financial resources be affected, but so will your time.

Talk to your spouse or partner and if children are involved, you may also want to include them in the decision-making process. With health insurance, life insurance and other expenses, you want to make sure that you have safety nets in place before you start.

As someone who never mastered double Dutch as a child, I now realize that starting anything that is difficult is often more of a mental decision than just a physical one. Going from freelancing on the side to freelancing full-time and using it as a springboard to start a business has been one of the most difficult, yet fulfilling things that I have ever done.

So, just like the game of Double Dutch, get prepared and jump in when you are ready.

Believing in Your Idea

Many of us see entrepreneurship as an opportunity to be autonomous, independent, and to fully use our gifts and talents. It is a cornerstone of the American way and for many, it is an opportunity to fully partake in some version of the American Dream.

With all of its merits and potential for personal and financial growth, there is also a side to entrepreneurship that many of us don't think about before we begin: Are you prepared to deliver the level of consistency that entrepreneurship and self-employment require?

If there is a hierarchy of things to consider, consistency would be one of the most important prerequisites for success. No matter how skilled you are or how innovative your services or products, you must be consistent with the effort that you put forth and with the quality of your work.

Why Consistency Matters

I once met an aspiring freelancer who was launching her career as a social media strategist. As a strategist, her tasks included creating content, copywriting, and distributing content on social media to generate a buzz and/or to influence sales. She reached out to me because she was ready to take her business to the next level, and she wanted me to introduce her services to some of my clients who had very large social media platforms and followings.

At first, she was sharing content on a daily basis. The content was well written and definitely of a high quality. She then shifted to posting every other day and then to once a week. Over time, her page stopped coming through my newsfeed, so I assumed that it was a new FB algorithm. I went to her business page to check it out.

It was May; her last post was from January. In essence, the page was dormant, so I reached out to her to make sure that she was ok. She informed me that she had become so busy with a PR project for another client that she couldn't consistently update the page. Ironically, she planned to outsource her page's maintenance and content development to someone else.

Although it was her right to shift gears, it didn't bode well for her brand or her reputation as a social media strategist. I wanted to support her and I planned to use her services and recommend her to one of my clients. But I couldn't take the risk that she would not follow through or that she would manage our pages the way that she had managed her own.

When a freelancer is inconsistent, it can leave potential clients with doubts about whether or not their project will receive the time, attention, and expertise that it deserves. With the aforementioned example, I am just one potential client who she missed out on. I'd assume, in light of her business, there were probably others.

The Long-term Value of Being Consistent
The end goal of having a sustainable and profitable business is doable. The key is treating each project as if it is important, because it is. Whether you have been in business for one month or for twenty years, your level of consistency is a reflection of your craftsmanship and how much you value your clients. It also helps others to build trust and respect for you and for your work.

I can't speak for all entrepreneurs, but many of the ones that I have worked with or who I have taken on as clients have shared anecdotes about the importance of their clients knowing that the quality and caliber of their work is dependable. If they said that a product would be ready by a certain date, it was. If they advertised a certain caliber of product, they delivered it. Consistency, in turn, keeps clients coming back and leads to word-of-mouth referrals.

Stay On Your Path
For many, entrepreneurship can be a pathway to professional

happiness. If you're seriously considering taking the leap, make sure that you have the time, energy, and stamina to make a consistent effort with your craft. It is tempting to take shortcuts, to cut corners, and to get complacent, but, in the end, all of the marketing in the world is not an antidote to inconsistency.

It may take a few tries before you figure out what works best for you, but when you do, keep doing it. There is an old adage that, "You have to pay the cost to be the boss." This cost is not just the financial capital that is necessary to run a business but the cost that revolves around giving your best effort every time.

You Can Stand Out in a World that Values Conformity

Since the 2016 election, I have seen people unfriend people, block them, and engage in some of the most contentious conversations on social media. Some are rejoicing that America will be made great (again) and others lament that this is the end of the world as we know it.

I have even seen some people comment that they are dreading the upcoming Thanksgiving season because of the cumbersome task of having to sit at the same table with family members who have diametrically opposed political views. Yes, unfortunately, this is not hyperbole.

As I watch people volley back and forth, I can't help but to think about those of us who are freelancers or creative entrepreneurs. In a world that is becoming increasingly more polarized, what is our role? Is there a place for creativity, for humanity in the political volcano that is erupting?

The resounding answer is yes! Not only is there a place for us, our roles have become even more important and relevant.

Think about your favorite song, piece of artwork, book, play, or musical. What draws you into that space? For me, the arts are a sanctuary. I can get lost in the words on a page, a melody playing in my ear or the pure simplicity of seeing a piece of artwork.

Behind each of those creations is someone who had a vision for his/her artistic expression. The manifestation of that is then enjoyed and consumed by others. Paradoxically, some of the best art is born out of, or explores, times of peril, injustice, pain and yes, political unrest and strife.

As creative entrepreneurs, our task is not to put our blinders on and pretend as if we live in a bubble where politics don't affect us, our viability as artists, or our creative expression. As many women avowed in the 1970s, "The personal is political."

We can't get away from this nor should we.

My bias runs deep, not because I am a writer, but because the arts, literature in particular, helped to shape my worldview. I place the arts right up there with religion, education, and family when it comes to the things that I value the most.

You see, I am not Irish, but *Angela's Ashes* taught me about extreme poverty in Ireland in the 1930s and 1940s. I have never experienced life-threatening financial deprivation, but *Grapes of Wrath* helped me to understand pure desperation. I do not have any learning disabilities, but *Of Mice and Men* taught me to have empathy for those who do. I was never an enslaved African woman, but Incidents in the Life of a Slave Girl provided me with a lens to understand her physical, emotional and psychological pain.

Like many others, I experience cultures other than my own through art for art has allowed me to understand life beyond my lived experiences. Most importantly, literature made me more empathetic and taught me how to engage in civil discourse. I may not agree with people's political views, but I am not going to annihilate them in order to prove my point.

What I see in post-election America right now is frightening and this has nothing to do with a particular political party or the President-elect, but everything to do with the reality that having authentic and healthy conversations across religious, socioeconomic, and racial lines may be too idealistic right now. Too many of us are operating in fear and that fear is usurping our ability to feel.

So what can we do? We do what great artists, writers, musicians, and other creative spirits have done generations before us—we operate in our gifts.

In a 2015 *Nation* article, Toni Morrison, reminded us, "This is precisely the time when artists go to work. There is no time for despair, no place for self-pity, no need for silence, no room for fear. We speak, we write, we do language. That is how civilizations heal."

Not only does someone need your book, your song, your art, your play, or your musical, someone may need it now more than ever.
My pen is my protest—what's yours?

Love Can Be The Guiding Force of Your Business

When we think of passion, compassion, and even love, we may associate these words with romantic or familial relationships. Rarely do we link these terms to business.

When is the last time that you heard someone say any of the following?

I am in love with my company.
I am passionate about sharing my goods and services with the world.
I demonstrate compassion when interfacing with my clients.

Yes, those sentences may have some difficulty rolling off of your tongue or springing from your lips. Somehow, they just don't seem to belong in a discussion about business or business practices.

But shouldn't they?

We tend to be guided by higher principals when we are motivated or driven by love; I know I am. This is why I make a point of telling people how much I love my clients; I also tell my team how much I love them. Yes, it's corny, but they know me well enough to also know that it's true.

Years before I even thought about starting my own company, I served as a teaching assistant for a Business Communication course at the William E. Simon School of Business at the University of Rochester. In the cutthroat world that was top-ranked business school culture in the 1990s, I had to navigate an ecosystem that was incredibly foreign and uncomfortable at times. I saw students who refused to help each other; I listened in on class discussions that revolved around case studies where toxic waste had been illegally dumped into poor communities by Fortune 500 companies.

Because the proper clean-up would affect the companies' bottom line and hurt stock prices, many students argued that the companies had done the right thing—I listened in horror as MBA candidates justified this and put price tags on human lives, lives that they deemed less significant and valuable than their own. Everything seemed to revolve around greed and self-indulgence.

I am sure these students all evolved into wonderful captains of industry, but it left me with a very sour taste in my mouth. After I finished my year-long obligation, I said that I would never go into business. Ever!

Fast forward almost 13 years, and I found myself filling out the paperwork for an LLC. From day one, I said that my company would be driven by purpose and not profit. I admit that there was an element of naïveté. For a while, I would render services for free or discount them so deeply that there was no profit margin.

Like others who are deeply passionate about the work that we create, I had some difficulty understanding that art and commerce could co-exist. It did not have to be an either/or dichotomy. Some of my writing was art and it had tangible value; therefore, there was nothing wrong with being compensated for it.

I've been thinking about this quite a bit as I think about the future of entrepreneurship in America. As with any business endeavor, many of us want to be profitable, but we also want compassion to be a cornerstone of what we do. Practically anybody can make money, but how you make your money and what you compromise to do it are equally as important.

My daddy used to say, "All money isn't good money." In my youthful jubilance, I challenged that assertion as I thought about what I could do with all of that not-so-good money. My father, who was stern and stoic, would simply listen to my retort and remind me that I still had a lot of living to do. He was right. I had a sophomoric view of money and financial matters because, to be honest, I was comfortable. We tend not to think about things until they become deeply personal or relevant.

The first time I witnessed the dark side of business practices—where everything had a price tag with little, to no regard, for the human consequences—I initially froze. Until you see it up close, it's just theory or a case study in a book. For me, it was not worth it and I walked away from what would have been, at the time, my most lucrative contract.

The reality is that most of us who are either freelancing or small business owners have not taken business ethics courses; we do not have MBAs; instead, we are building our planes as we fly them. Because of this, we have to be careful because unethical business practices can be subtle. For entrepreneurs, this tends to happen when we come across a practice, a business opportunity, or a potential partnership whose purpose or mission is incongruent with ours.

Ideally, all of our financial interfaces would be mission aligned, but sometimes, they can be mission adrift and that's when you really have to think about whether the bottom line is really worth it.

Believe that Your Gift Will Make Room For You

A few years ago, I gave a lecture for National Women's Equality Day and much of my presentation centered around what it means to be empowered. Even though my speech was about women's empowerment and the ratification of the 19th Amendment, it made me wonder how empowerment can be applied when addressing the world of freelancing.

So, I embarked upon a quest to find a definition of empowerment that would be most applicable to the freelancing industry—with some tweaking, as I will explain later.

Business Dictionary defines empowerment as follows: "A management practice of sharing information, rewards, and power with employees so that they can take the initiative and make decisions to solve problems and improve service and performance."

Empowerment is based on the idea that giving employees skills, resources, authority, opportunity, motivation, as well as holding them responsible and accountable for outcomes of their actions, will contribute to their competence and satisfaction. Obviously, this definition is predicated upon a traditional employee/employer model, but there are still some aspects of this that are useful when talking about being empowered as an entrepreneur.

Why is this important? Feeling empowered can lead to the stamina that you need to successfully pivot. It can also help you understand what kind of leader or manager you are.

Be clear about your style
This may seem odd because you may not be managing other people yet. However, if you are in business, you are managing not only your time, but also your skills, your resources, and your finances. Think about some of the managerial-like decisions that you have made about your freelancing career. What was the impetus for your decision making?

There is a strong probability that your style determined the way you make decisions. The key to empowerment is having a working understanding of your style and the best situations to apply it to. A few years ago, The Huffington Post presented a concise and user-friendly article about management style. You may find it helpful to peruse it and determine if one of the six management styles is closest to yours. Keep in mind that managerial styles will vary from person to person, or situation to situation, so be clear about what works best for you in your industry.

Create measurable outcomes
How will you know if your idea will work? Have you set your goals yet? Goal-setting is a well-tested mechanism to create an external layer of accountability. It moves beyond just intrinsic motivation and hones in on concrete and measurable outcomes.

Think of this as your personal growth plan. There are things that you have already accomplished that are replicable; they were not by default, but by design. The key is putting a name to them, being specific and being clear about timelines for accomplishment. Instead of someone else checking to see if you have accomplished these outcomes, assess yourself.

Reward yourself
When is the last time that you literally rewarded yourself because you accomplished or exceeded a goal? Incentive pay and merit pay are not that uncommon in traditional industries, but it may seem odd to think about it as a freelancer. But, it makes sense. You have positioned yourself to be successful, so why not reward your own efforts?

Inspiration can come in different forms. For some, a reward may be a dinner at a favorite restaurant or for others, it may be splurging on a vacation.

It doesn't really matter what the reward is—it matters that you see yourself as being actively involved in your own satisfaction with freelancing. Sure, there are aspects of this that you cannot control, but this one you certainly can.

Will there be times when being an entrepreneur is disempowering? *Yes.* Will there be moments when you wish you were more empowered? *Yes.*

Unfortunately, I have personally seen people low-ball start-ups because the assumption was that 'some work is better than no work' or that a person working for him/herself is desperate for work.

Obviously, this is not true, but I am sure that all of us have accepted a contract or job for which we were underpaid or for which our hourly rate was low. This is the antithesis of feeling empowered.

It's important that you frequently evaluate your practices to determine what, if anything, needs to be tweaked or retooled. This may necessitate acquiring tools, resources or training that will enable you to grow or expand as a freelancer.

The Steps You Can Take Now To Make Sure that Your Idea Works

If nothing else, the last decade has shown us what can happen when people come together to work towards a common goal. Whether it is political, social, cultural, or economic concerns, working collaboratively has led to measurable change and, for many, this is just the beginning. The same can be true for you. Whether it's using your social media platforms, personal relationships, or networks, people like you are positively influencing other people simply by using your voice.

As you become more comfortable with a business idea or concept, you will begin to see how it can translate from something in your imagination to something that is tangible. In this day of digitization, the key is to be and to stay informed. The dissemination of information is often the first step in actualizing an idea. The more you know about what's going on, the better equipped you are to lend your voice to issues and problems that are important to you. Most successful businesses solve problems or a need.

Support Businesses that are Similar to the One You Want to Start
I personally have a vested interest in the success of others. Why? Because I see myself as a part of a larger body that is changing the narrative of what it means to be successful in America. In other words, entrepreneurship is often a pathway to economic freedom. As such, I want my fellow entrepreneurs to win.

Before I became one, I supported small business owners. I also learned as much as I could about my industry. I studied case studies and explored people who were doing well and those who were not successful.

This means that from the start, I deliberately set out to support others. To this day, I work with other freelancers, small business owners and contract workers on projects; I hire them; and I often make referrals. This may all seem inconsequential, but the more you deliberately and actively engage in this level of support of others, the more others will support you.

I firmly believe that by engaging in work that is authentic for you, you will attract the people and the resources that you need to build your idea.

Be Willing To Get Your Feet Wet
Before I started Seldon Writing Group, LLC, I didn't give much thought to this. Now that I fully grasp the idiosyncrasies of it, I understand that $500 spent with a major corporation is probably not going to mean as much as it does for someone whose livelihood depends upon the support of people like you and me.

As an added benefit of this patronage, the quality, craftsmanship, and customer service are often exceptional because for many entrepreneurs, our livelihood is contingent upon the support of others.

In 2008, I was working full time as a university department chair at a university that was up for reaccreditation. In addition to teaching, hiring new faculty, advising, and engaging in a university-wide self-study, I was actively involved in my church and with the alumnae chapter of my sorority. My life was, to say the least, very busy.

Paradoxically, it was during one of the busiest points in my life that I started actively thinking about starting a company. A local content creator asked me to contribute to a national, multicultural resource curriculum. My first thought was to decline because the idea of adding one more thing to my schedule seemed impossible. But the project was so compelling that I eventually said 'yes.' It would end up being one of the most comprehensive and rewarding freelancing projects that I have ever done.

Fast forward to 2019 and a dear friend from graduate school reached out to me on Facebook. She's a full-time professor who loves to write and she wants to explore freelancing. However, she's not sure how to fit it into her life. So, not surprisingly, shortly after catching up, she asked me: How do I make time to write?

Good question. After working a 40 to 45-hour work week in addition to one's other responsibilities, it may be incredibly difficult to see how freelancing can fit into an already busy and hectic schedule. Realistically, we can't manufacture more time, so how does one find time?

Not only is this a fair question, it's not necessarily an easy one to answer; however, there are some pragmatic steps that most people can take to integrate their business idea into their lives, even if they are still working a 9 to 5.

Be Realistic About your Time Commitments

Most of us are creatures of habit, which makes it plausible to forecast the amount of time that we spend on our various commitments. Because freelancing can (and should) be something that you enjoy and find value in doing, you don't want it to compete with your pre-existing commitments.

I highly recommend that you start with smaller freelance projects that I affectionately call 'one and done.' This simply means that you commit to one project at a time until you can get a sense of how freelancing fits into your life. As you get acclimated to meeting deadlines and unpacking the complexity of freelancing projects, you can either increase or decrease the number of projects that you commit to doing.

Carve out Time to Hone in on Your Craft

I often tell my mentees and clients that you have to set aside time to write. If you think of it as an ongoing commitment like a university class, lesson, or an event then there is a greater possibility that you will show up.

At first, this may be difficult, but over time, you will find that you can actually reclaim more of your time because you are not overscheduling or overcommitting. For example, I don't schedule any appointments or sessions for Monday because that is my day to write. I have committed myself to a writing day and even on days when I am unmotivated and uninspired, I still write.

A full day may be unrealistic when you first start freelancing, so you may want to start in smaller increments like an hour or two. Whether it's daily, weekly, or bi-weekly, the key is to block out time on your calendar and work the rest of your schedule around your set-aside freelancing time. This will lead to greater consistency and discipline. In turn, it will free you up to take on additional projects.

Just Say No
If you are seriously committed to launching your freelancing career then you may have to give-up or sacrifice something else. The good news is that you don't have to make a life-altering change, you just may need to rethink how you are parceling out your time. And this may simply boil down to saying no.

As simple as it sounds, saying no, especially for those of us who are entrepreneurial in spirit, may be difficult. Yet, it is often necessary. As I think back over how I managed my life back in 2008, I realize that I started to be more protective of my time.

Being successful as a freelancer was important to me and I wanted my work to reflect that. As such, I literally had to prioritize freelancing over some other activities. Freelancing compared to some of the other things in my life was not only enjoyable, but it also brought value to my life. This, in turn, meant that I had to let some of those other things go.

From that first major project in 2008 to 2019, what, at one time, seemed to be impossible not only became possible but an intricate part of my life.

Although these are small steps, over time, you should be able to dedicate more time to freelancing.

2

[I MESSED UP]
THE VALUE OF MAKING MISTAKES

There are years that ask questions and years that answer.

-Zora Neale Hurston

One of the reasons why many of our ideas don't launch, have false starts, or they orbit in a perpetual limbo state is because we have unrealistic expectations about how things should work out for us. There is this misnomer that perfection or getting things right are the only ways to grow or get better. I'd like to disrupt that mode of thinking by suggesting that our mistakes, our failures, and yes, our mess ups actually make us better at our craft.

For many years, I was a closeted writer. I would write, but my musings were intended exclusively for an audience of one—me. I was not so much concerned about my writing skills; instead, I was afraid that my writing was not good enough because my voice didn't matter.

This was compounded by the fact that after numerous submissions to various publications and outlets, I was met with the "After Careful Consideration" letter or, as I preferred to call it, the "This Sucks" letter. Perhaps, the fear of rejection also stems back to a bad experience that I had as an undergrad when one of my professors questioned why I wanted to be a Black English major (I will save that story for another book) or maybe it was my own insecurities about my grammar skills, or lack thereof.

Whatever the cause, the fear of being rejected was paralyzing, so much so that I often hid behind the fact that I was a teacher of writing and not actually a writer.

Looking back, this seems like such an arbitrary distinction because it was. Simply put, this was just an excuse to justify my not trying. At least with not trying to write for the public, I could never fail. Like many writers, failure is more than just an empty, nebulous term. It is the boogeyman of writing. Just because it doesn't have a definitive shape doesn't mean that it doesn't exist.

When I taught writing, I often encountered students who were also afraid to write. Their trepidation was not a result of poor writing skills, but often a lack of confidence. Frequently, this was an outgrowth of their unwillingness to be vulnerable or to trust the people who were reading their writing. It didn't matter if it was a freshman introductory English class or a senior thesis seminar, this pattern emerged across grade-levels and abilities.

Since my time as an English professor, I have encountered aspiring writers and even established professional writers who find themselves combating self-doubt and fear. As much as I would like to think that this is just a function of one's nerves, it seems to be more nuanced than that. Writing is personal; writing is subjective and on numerous occasions, I have argued that writing truly is an extension of one's soul. So what happens when one's writing is rejected, criticized, or ridiculed?

It feels personal, so many of us take it personally. You see there is a certain level of intimacy that takes place when a writer picks up the, literal or metaphoric, pen. Ideas that were once isolated to one's thoughts, one's imagination and one's worldview are transformed in a way that others will have to understand and interact with them. And, yes, criticize them.

Ideally, a reader will understand your written words as if he/she were privy to your most intimate thoughts. But, too often, this may not happen—at least not that perfectly. It seems that the difference between those who keep going and those who don't is confidence—not so much the belief that one is a great writer, but the belief that one's ideas are worthy of being heard and that there is an audience that needs to hear them.

People value honesty. Of course a lucid, compelling, and engaging story will generate reads, but there is something about reading the works of authors who are naked that invites us to keep reading, to beg for more, and to become a fan. It is a steep learning curve writing for an audience of strangers. It is an even deeper dive learning how to receive and even invite criticism. I suspect this applies to other freelancing fields as well.

Rejection has been good—really good—because it has taught me that I have to get better at my craft. Freelancing is competitive and there are some seriously brilliant people out there who have put in their 10,000 hours of "deliberate practice" as Malcolm Gladwell implores all of us to do in Outliers.

Had I been successful early on, I don't think that I would enjoy writing as much. It is still challenging and I am still mindful that my writing is consumable, so I owe it to my audience to have something worthwhile and useful to say.

So my advice for anyone who is wavering between freelance writing and the fear of freelance writing is to write and to embrace the journey. Like many other professions, it is feedback and the criticism from others that makes us better.

But, Isn't the Idea Perfection?

I recently had an intense conversation with a client—the kind that lingers long after you've hung up the phone. He is an entrepreneur, and we were discussing his recent book project and how it didn't quite turn out the way he planned. It wasn't as perfect of a process as he envisioned it would be.

Great expectations
He expected blockbuster sales, great reviews, and a jump to the top of someone's bestseller list. Because these things did not happen within an allocated time period, he rationalized that book writing wasn't in his wheelhouse and that he would probably retire his newly-inked pen.

The next morning, I thought about my client and I started reflecting upon one of my father's favorite expressions: "Slow and steady wins the race." I posted it on my Instagram page and I shared how, as a child, I had a tendency to start/stop many projects or activities if they either took too long or the results were not immediately satisfactory.

Patience pays off
My dad would often warn me that I was developing a poor life habit and that I needed to be patient and to focus more on the long-term results. Although he didn't know it, he was preparing me for life as a freelancer and as a small business owner. Through his constant repetition of the phrase and his using it as a springboard for a series of cautionary tales, he was instilling in me the importance of both longevity and sustainability. He was also helping me to redefine what it means to win.

Those lessons are even more important today because many of us are primed to think that success is an outgrowth of simply trying. If you work hard enough you will succeed. Pull yourself up by your own bootstraps. If person A could do it then so can you. I literally cringe when I see these sayings and memes come through my newsfeed. Why?

Go your own way
Because there is a meta-narrative that emerges that can be hurtful and

detrimental to aspiring freelancers and entrepreneurs: Success (however defined) should be immediate and if you are not successful then something must be wrong with you.

The reality is that staying the course and pushing through the rough patches and difficult aspects of being self-employed or freelancing are just as important as being able to tout having 1000 customers, high-value clients, or six-figure earnings.

Sure, these may be earmarks of success, but how often do we ask: For every client that you now have, how many did you start with? For every $10,000 contract that you have signed, how many $100 contracts did you acquire along the way? For every well executed plan that you created, how many re-dos or do-overs came before it?

Strategies for success

There is a strong possibility that if you ask people how they were able to excel or become the best in their fields, they will probably tell you that their outputs were often the results of depersonalizing, processing, being patient and having a laser-sharp focus. Their success was not the result of being perfect.

We need to be honest with ourselves about this. Are there outliers and people who do experience immediate success and tremendous growth, all while executing something perfectly the first time? I am sure someone is out there, but this is probably just as rare as a unicorn in someone's backyard in suburban America.

Permission to be imperfect

In other words, in a world that makes being perfect the end goal, we need to give ourselves permission to be imperfect. Imperfect is not interchangeable with irresponsible, sloppy, imprudent, reckless, or even undependable; it simply means that there will be times throughout this journey that you will mess up; you will need a second chance; and you will need to start over.

And that is perfectly ok. In fact, it's beautiful. It is often in the trenches and in the weeds that we truly understand how things work and what we need to do to improve our craft and enhance our process.

Like my client, other entrepreneurs, mentees, and friends who are on the cusp of quitting something, or second guessing it, I leave you with the words of artist Erin Hanson:

> "There is freedom waiting for you,
> On the breezes of the sky,
> And you ask 'What if I fall?'
> Oh but my darling,
> What if you fly?"

Like many of you who are reading this, when I first started my business, I was ambitious and I was driven. I was also foolish. I erroneously thought that my way of doing things was the best way until I made one of the biggest mistakes of my freelancing career. It was a mistake that would ultimately cost me a client, but it was also a mistake that led to some of the most valuable lessons that I have learned to date.

While I was still working full-time, I freelanced on the side. It was not only a great way to supplement my income, but it was fun and a nice break from the rigors of teaching. A colleague reached out to me and asked me if I would be willing to edit her husband's first book. I said sure. At that time, most of my freelancing was writing related, curriculum writing to be specific. But I also had experience copyediting curriculum and academic texts. So, foraying into the world of editing a full-length nonfiction text seemed doable.

The mistake
I connected with her husband; we settled on a mutually agreeable price and executed a contract. I jumped right in. Before I knew it, there was more red ink on his manuscript than black. Upon completing it, I sent it to my client and anxiously awaited his response. To say that I was excited would be an understatement.

The next day, I received an email. My client was livid that I had co-opted his voice and his book was no longer his. He claimed that I had over-corrected the text to the point that he felt as if I had coauthored the book instead of edited it.

As I read the email over and over again, I was floored by his caustic and accusatory tone. I thought I had done an excellent job. Prepared to defend my actions and to stand behind my work. I typed up a lengthy e-mail response and hit send. And then, empathy kicked in.

The "remedy"
What if I were him? Rather than maintaining a defensive stand, I stepped back so that I could see things through his eyes. It had taken him two years to write the book and it was deeply personal in nature. By handing his work over to me, he was entrusting me to maintain the integrity of his voice while simultaneously lending my technical expertise to his written text.

Indeed, I had taken too many liberties with his text. He had intentionally used some vernacular and colloquial language, not because he didn't know any better [he was a highly esteemed lawyer], but because that was his writing style for that particular text. It was his choice. As an editor, instead of assuming that it was incorrect, I should have asked or sought clarification. In other words, with a few extra steps, this tense interaction could have been avoided.

I did, subsequently, offer to remedy the problem by re-editing the book; he declined. Instead, he reiterated his disappointment in my work and we never corresponded after that. Even his wife became more distant. Eventually, I did receive an email, along with 500 other people, announcing that the book had been published. I felt awful that I couldn't truly celebrate this milestone—the first full-length text that I edited and his first book.

The lessons learned
It has been close to seven years since this happened and paradoxically, I am glad that this happened relatively early in my freelancing career. Had I continued with the *I am right* and *I know better than you* mentality then I definitely would not be in business. As with most things that force us to lean into discomfort and to re-evaluate our actions, I became a better freelancer and a better, more attuned, editor.

This mea culpa experience taught me the importance of being clear with my clients about their expectations before we begin. In many instances, clients know exactly what they want. In other instances, when they are uncertain or indifferent, I make recommendations or suggestions. The recommendations are specific and clear. More than anything, this helps to mitigate unmet or unrealistic expectations.

Maintaining relationships
Another valuable lesson that I learned was the importance of building and maintaining relationships. All of the money in the world is not worth getting the reputation of being difficult, incompetent, or uncaring. Although I cared deeply about my client's project, I can understand, as I later found out, why he thought our interaction was purely transactional. I do wonder if he would have become a long-term client if I had handled things differently. As a client reminded me this week, it's impossible to have a second chance at doing something right the first time.

And perhaps the greatest lesson is one that applies to all who have an idea that we want to nurture and grow: Remember that your clients are entrusting you with something that they care deeply about; if not, they would not be investing their time and resources in seeking your services. We can always add new skills to our arsenal, but the extra time it takes to be patient, to listen, and to empathize can lead to a lifetime of happy clients and excellent service.

Don't Try to Do Everything—Why Outsourcing May be The Answer

It never fails to happen: When I reconnect with a former student or colleague, the question of, "So, what are you up to these days?" comes up. Such was the case about five years ago when I met with a former student for breakfast. My company was still in the start-up phase. After filling her in, she asked: "Would you do it [start your own company] again?"

The question was innocuous enough, but it did cause me to pause. Rarely, if ever, does anyone ask me that. I guess because most of my peers are my age, they understand the nuances of secondary and even tertiary career shifts, but looking into the eyes of a bright-eyed, corporate, 25-year old melted a layer of defensiveness and I answered as honestly as I could.

"Yes, but there are so many things that I wish someone had told me before I started freelancing." And thus, our conversation became the inspiration for this vignette.

When contemplating the world of entrepreneurship, many of us think about the freedom that comes with it, the flexibility of working from home or a coffee shop, and the ability to carve out a work/life balance that some of us never experienced in previous lives. I loved the idea of being able to write and being able to work remotely, literally, from anywhere.

Yet, for all of the joys of doing this work, there are a few egregious missteps that I made and that I have seen others make that can be avoided by having a firm understanding of the following: Doing-It-Yourself (DIY) may work for building a trench in the backyard or adding a backsplash in a kitchen, but you may want to rethink DIY when it comes to being a business owner, especially during the ideation stage.

Prior to leaving an anchor institution, my experiences revolved around teaching others the joys of reading and interpreting literature and the merits of expressing oneself in writing. Throw in a few ancillary responsibilities and that was the extent of my professional life. All of my degrees are in English. I never took a business class—not even as an undergraduate. I never had to. My entire life was mapped out by someone's HR department, accounts payable office and business management team. Understandably, and perhaps arrogantly, my biggest concern was with keeping up with my bi-weekly paycheck.

The minute I transitioned from being paid by someone else to paying myself, my world turned topsy turvy. Suddenly, spending hundreds of dollars on a purse seemed foolish. Treating my friends to an elaborate dinner, just because, became a bad investment. And getting a new car simply because that year's model had an extra exhaust pipe became laughable. In other words, I started to see money, my spending, and my professional aspirations through a different lens.

For the first few years, I struggled because I only wanted to focus on the creative side of writing. I wanted to create art for art's sake. In the meanwhile, I still had fiscal responsibilities that needed to be met. Stressing about paying my bills and keeping the lights on created anxiety and stress and before I knew it, my writing suffered.
DIY was going horrible wrong.

After almost finding myself in financial ruin and on the cusp of looking for a full-time job, I did what I should have done from day one. I finally came clean with myself and admitted that I did not fully grasp the commerce side of writing. My business acumen was in need of retooling and I needed help in doing so. Being a neophyte freelancer was like being a one-woman business entity without understanding the rules of engagement.

I started to study my industry. How much did other writers and editors charge? I discovered that I was not charging enough. I met with my accountant and we began projecting my 12-month cash flow: costs, expenses, revenues, and shortfalls. With the advice of legal counsel, we created contracts, invoices, and other documents. At the advice of another friend, I started leveraging the LLC that I created years before—although this may not be a viable option for all. I also started an email list and learned the value of branding and promoting my freelance writing on social media.

I started reading books by business industry leaders and I even took a few online self-study classes for entrepreneurs. My right brain lamented that she was tired of my left brain getting all of the attention.

Having an infrastructure and a team has turned everything around. I am still learning, but now, I really can focus on my craft because I have a system in place that allows me to ebb and flow as a freelancer.

There are those who may believe that once freelancing starts to feel like a pseudo-corporation then you are no longer a real freelancer—somehow the essence of your craft is diluted. From my personal experience, that train of thought actually pushes some of us back into traditional jobs. It prevents well-meaning entrepreneurs from fully embracing their ability to benefit from the commerce side of their art.

Instead of creating an arbitrary either/or dichotomy, I have another suggestion, especially for writers: You can practice your craft, be impassioned about your subject matter and get compensated for your writing—just be careful of DIY all by yourself.

Not Everyone Will Believe in Your Idea

In an ideal context, I would start this section of the book by telling you that your family and immediate circle of friends will believe in and pour into your idea. However, this may not be true, so you need to be prepared. Unfortunately, those support systems may have to go beyond our friends and family members, especially if they don't understand the complexities of freelancing. To this day, I still have some people who ask me, "When do you plan to go back to a real job? Or "Why would you walk away from such a stable career?"—as if a midlife crisis has propelled me into the world of entrepreneurship. Trust me, it hasn't. Yet, there were times, especially early on when I doubted my ability to fully execute my idea.

The first time that I was asked to blog for a national outlet, I was afraid. I wasn't afraid because I doubted my writing skills or the subject that I was tackling. My fear was precipitated by the vast unknown that we call the internet.

As an avid reader, I was accustomed to how easily and frequently people would comment on others' written pieces. Some of the comments were thoughtful and engaging; conversely, others were outright virulent and borderline evil.

Rather than focusing on a positive outcome, I allowed myself to go "there." The "there" that hones in on someone else challenging and critiquing my writing. Like many writers, I believe that writing is an extension of one's soul. So, from a metaphysical perspective, I perceived an attack on my writing as an attack on Tyra. As some writers have pointed out "the personal is the political".

Well, the first blog was well received and before I knew it, I was blogging more frequently and fervently. In essence, I loved it. Until that one day that I wrote about a polarizing topic. Actually, in hindsight, it was a thoughtful topic that happened to have an enticing title, evoking the name of popular rapper and music mogul Jay-Z.

I thought that I had been neutral enough and that the readership would read closely enough to walk away with some hearty food for thought. Buoyantly, I read the comments. Nodding my head in agreement, I beamed with pride as many of the readers expressed positive sentiments. Then I started encountering the "Who does she think she is?" and "What makes her an expert?" type of comments.

Clearly, I was the *she* that they were referring to. My first inclination was to respond with a long laundry list of my credentials and work in the community. I remember calling my mentor who had introduced me to the blogosphere and his response was concise and matter of fact, "Don't read the comments." I tried to convince him that somehow, I had been wronged and that I needed to defend my honor and his stance remained the same, "Don't read the comments."

After that I shied away from polemical material and focused on feel good and middle of the road blog topics. In other words, I let fear get the best of me. Looking back, I was pretty melodramatic, but the point remains the same: I limited my opportunities to write because of a fear factor. In fact, fear overtook me.

Had I allowed that early experience to frame how I saw my gift and my idea to write professionally then I wouldn't be where I am today. My point is that you have to believe so confidently in your idea that you are willing to work hard for it and stand firmly on the fertile ground that you will be able to execute it.

You also have to be willing to grow, evaluate, and reinvent yourself as needed. Stagnation, comfort, and complacency are all idea killers.

So, whatever you are working on right now, I want you to think about what's holding you back. What is your greatest fear about executing your idea? Go ahead and name it. Naming something that is holding you back and being able to clearly identify what it is not only demystifies it, but it also takes away its power.

3

INVESTING IN YOURSELF

The difference between winning and losing is most often not quitting.

-Walt Disney

I live in a mid-size city that is known more for its sports prowess than it is known for its creative communities. I admit that I am slightly envious of some of my peers who live in larger areas with more diverse populations. In fact, I sometimes wonder if my writing would be enhanced if I could tap into the creative energy of other self-defined and professional writers in person.

One of the things that you want to do and do with great frequency is invest in yourself. Whether it is in-person or virtual, link up with a community that can serve as a support system when you need one.

When you are still chiseling out your idea, you will need to be around people who can listen, provide feedback and yes, offer valuable criticism. No one wants to start a project just for it to fail. Creative types who work alone often need to be reminded that they are not alone even if it feels like it at times.

Unlike conventional jobs that require "co-workers" to socialize, some entrepreneurial neophytes will have limited contact with people besides their clients. If there is one thing that you may miss about working for someone else or at an anchor institution, it is talking to and interfacing with other people on a daily basis.

Paradoxically, the things that used to annoy me the most are the things that I miss the most about being a member of a work community. Bouncing ideas off of one another, listening to stories about people's families and children, and talking politics while sipping on a warm cup of tea doesn't happen in my home office where I sit in front of computer screens most of the day.

This, I have found, can lead to a sense of isolation and, in some instances, frustration which is why it is so important that we are intentional and deliberate about having support systems.

But, to be honest, being disconnected can be a downside when you first start, but it doesn't have to be. I am sure many of us want to commune with like-minded people with whom we have shared experiences; it validates that we are not venturing down a road untraveled.

More importantly, there is nothing quite like being a part of a community where people "get you." You don't have to explain the nuances of your field or justify why self-employment is a better alternative to working for someone else.

Of course, I am not suggesting that you have to go create your own groups. In fact, I have noticed several Meetup opportunities for writers so this may be a viable option for you. Realistically, the joy that I experience doing the things that I am passionate about serves as a form of fuel that recharges me when I am on E (empty), so I can only imagine how connecting with other writers will add to that creative energy.

Seeing the Finish Line: Setting Realistic Goals

If you are like most people, you have probably set goals, made resolutions, or created a vision board for the upcoming year. Did you keep them? Why? Why not?

One of the most important things that you need to do during the ideation phase of your business is to set realistic, measurable goals. Before you do, reflect on how important it is for you to be successful. It is not enough to say, "I want to be profitable" or "I want more projects or clients." You must ask yourself: What is my plan of action? How do I convert my wants/needs into tangible outcomes?

I recommend that you first carve out a mission statement. Like the mission statement of a corporation or a not-for-profit, it is imperative that you have a clear purpose of who you are, what you do, and why you do it.

I have a mission statement that is about seven sentences long. It is a tangible reminder of how I see myself as a freelance writer. When I become mission adrift, I recalibrate. Like any written document, as you grow and as you evolve, so too will your mission so you can always tweak or revise it. It is a living and breathing document that is intended to anchor you.

Next, I suggest that you start with the finish line in focus. How do you want your fiscal or calendar year to end? No, you didn't misread that; I didn't say 'start.' Start with the finish line and not the starting line. Think about a marathon runner. Her objective isn't to start – it's to finish! The training that goes into preparing for a marathon is predicated on crossing the finish line. When I trained for a mini-marathon in 2012, we often did visualization exercises in addition to our physical training. I can honestly say that when I couldn't feel my feet at the 10-mile marker, it was imagining the finish line that pushed me through.

In education, this is called Understanding by Design (UbD). It was developed by Grant Wiggins and Jay McTighe. I frequently use UbD as a freelancer because it helps me to make sure that my actions are aligned to my goals.

The premise is pretty straight forward: In order to determine how you are going to tackle or accomplish something, your planning shouldn't start at the beginning; instead, you should start with your intended outcomes and work backwards. Because of this, some people have even called it backwards design. It may feel counterintuitive at first, but it works. And the reason that it works is because assessing your achievement is embedded throughout the process. Here's how you can apply this to the ideation stage:

Think about your desired results. Let's say that my desired outcomes for my first 3 years are as follows: increase my client roster, pitch new blog ideas, and write a book.

Specify. I assign specific attributes to each outcome. Increase my roster by 20 clients; pitch 3 blog ideas to 3 different outlets; and write a book about writing. Keep in mind that outcomes must be tangible and measurable. They are the finish line.

Evaluate each new opportunity in relation to your goal. As you are seeking freelance opportunities, circle back to your stated outcomes. Think about how, or if, this opportunity is moving you closer to your desired results. Then determine if the opportunity is aligned or adrift.

Monitor your progress. Throughout the year, measure your success (or failure) based upon how close you are to hitting your targets. If you find that you are far off and some of your goals were too ambitious, you can make slight adjustments, but it is important that you don't forsake your desired results.

Once you reach or eclipse a goal, you can add on to it or create a new one. Use your experiences to help you gauge and set next year's outcomes.

Understanding where you want to end up will help you to stay focused throughout the ideation stage. By deliberately and intentionally seeking out contracts or projects that are aligned with your mission, you will find that you are able to wed your purpose with your passion. It will also help you to grow as a freelancer.

Although I love serendipity and the idea of everything being organic, when being an entrepreneur is your livelihood, you have to make sure that you have infrastructures in place. Otherwise, it is too tempting to wander or spend too much time and energy doing things that are not productive.

If planning or projecting ahead for years at a time sounds too daunting or too rigid, map out your goals for quarters using this approach. The more you see your idea as being real and doable, the more you will continue to work and fight for it.

Burnout is a Dream Killer

"I am not sure if this is for me."

I could hear the angst in my friend's voice. After months of chasing leads and looking for new clients, she was running on E. She was ready to quit freelancing.

"We all experience burnout," I said reassuringly. "Remember, even Superman had Kryptonite."

She chuckled a little and agreed to take some time off to readjust.

It is not uncommon for entrepreneurs to hit a wall, which may be the result of unfulfilled promises, unpaid invoices, monthly shortfalls, saturated markets, and/or poor payment rates. It is enough to make the most seasoned person take a time out and even contemplate quitting.

Unfortunately, there is no way to forecast exactly when it is going to happen, but it happens. The key, ironically, is not attempting to avoid it, but to come up with coping strategies to help you deal with it when it does occur. Like Kryptonite to Superman or a heel to Achilles, we have to do our best to protect ourselves in uncertain and difficult times.

Too often in the pursuit of entrepreneurial freedom, we get lost in the process and the pursuit. It is not uncommon for some entrepreneurs to work 60 plus hours per week or odd hours. Have you ever noticed who else is up with you at 1:30 am or the messages that are timestamped at 4:30 am? I am even guilty of sending emails at 3:00 am assuming that my client would not get it until the next morning, only to get a reply within 10 minutes. After apologizing profusely to him, he reminded me that it was ok because he was up "working too."

There have even been occasions where entrepreneurs have been so engrossed in projects that they have forgotten to, or didn't have time to, eat.

Many of us are willing to go above and beyond because we are working for ourselves. The drive to be the owner instead of the employee creates not only passion and drive, but also an added kick of adrenaline to help us push through tight deadlines. It reminds me of Pinky and the Brain, who plotted to take over the world every day. Of course, this is a hyperbole, but some of us have lofty goals and we literally chisel away at them on a daily basis. Of course, there is nothing wrong with having dreams or chasing them. But at what cost?

Unfortunately, some of us sacrifice our well-being and are in perpetual Hamster-on-a-wheel mode. We are moving, but we aren't going anywhere. When this happens, ask yourself: When is the last time that I did something for me? Not my career, not my family, not my friends, and not my community, but simply for me because I deserve it. If it helps, start keeping a log or journal of how many hours a week you spend on you versus on other people.

For many of us, we are goal-driven overachievers who have found a way to convert our skills, talents, and gifts into profitable enterprises. The thought of slowing down or stopping may seem oxymoronic, but it is necessary. I find that burnout often occurs when we don't have the stamina to keep up at our current pace or we are engaging in practices that are not sustainable. Let's be honest, operating on 3 to 4 hours of sleep is not optimal, yet some of us do it on a daily basis.

My antidote is self-care. Take the time to do things that refuel you. Be around people who care deeply about you and not just your success. Go to a movie, go see a play, do a weekend get-a-way, and/or play outside. And my favorite cure for burnout is to make sure that you laugh frequently and authentically. I am a pretty serious person and I sometimes write about heavy topics, but I invite humor into my life because it feeds my soul.

If you spend much of your time pouring into others—as most of us do—it's just a matter of time before you will feel depleted and burnt out. You cannot be your best self or do your best work if you are not in a good space, especially if you are a creative entrepreneur.

The key, for me, is being proactive and not reactive to the demands of entrepreneurship. Once you sense that you are losing vigor, it's time to rethink your action plan.

I do three things that have worked quite well: 1) step back, 2) reevaluate and 3) re-prioritize. In other words, tackle the things that are most time sensitive and urgent then make a plan for everything else, keeping in mind that you need to set aside some time for you. If it is appropriate and the project calls for it, lean on others to help you with it or see if someone in your support system can help you with your other responsibilities so that you can place your attention elsewhere.

I plan to circle back with my friend next week. I don't believe that she is going to quit. In fact, I know that she loves freelancing, she's just hit a wall. My hope is that she will either climb over it or find a way around it.

Winning the Tug-of-War Between Work and Life

During the ideation stage, you have to be particularly careful about prioritizing. Specifically, work/life balance tends to be one of the reasons that many of us enter into freelancing and entrepreneurship. On the outside looking in, it may seem as if there is parity between our work lives and our personal lives. Yet, by leaning in closer, one may discover that work/life balance can be equally as difficult for those of us who are self-employed as it is for those who are traditionally employed.

Why?

Because neither our home nor professional lives are always predictable, linear, logical or fair. Deals fall through; contracts aren't signed; and balances may be past due. Compound that with unexpected illnesses, the death of a family member, or an unexpected life-event and some entrepreneurs find themselves in quite the conundrum, not sure how to prioritize or how to determine what has to give.

And it's for this reason that sometimes our desire to put equal time and energy into our work life and our personal life may feel like an endless and tenuous game of tug-of-war—one of my least favorite games growing up. Besides the inevitable sore palms and aching arms, there was always the looming sense that there were never any real winners, just a bunch of sore kids with one group having earned bragging rights for the rest of the school year.

Game aside, the seriousness of finding balance doesn't relegate it to the same designation as that of a children's game, but it does call into question why we sometimes pit two things that are equally valuable—work and life—against each other. The reality is that they can be complimentary and not contending forces. So, here are a few simple strategies that you may want to consider in order to create that balance:

1. **Set Office Hours**—Whether you work remotely, in a co-space environment, or even in a brick and mortar space, you may want to consider establishing set office hours. There tends to be this misnomer that entrepreneurs are available 24/7. Although you may have great flexibility and adaptability, structure is still important to your longevity in the industry. Set office hours signal to your clients when you are available and more importantly, it frees you up to have a life outside of work.

2. **Say 'no'**—I have written about this before and it is worth repeating it in this blog: Say 'no' to_____ (fill in the blank). Saying "no" may be incredibly difficult, especially when you are first starting and you are trying to build up your clientele and/or establish your brand. The sooner you become comfortable saying *no*, or at least having criteria for when a request requires a 'no' answer, then the better off you will be in the long haul as those requests start to multiply or they become more time consuming. The good news is that saying 'no' to one thing frees you up to say 'yes' to something else—that other thing may or may not be work related.

3. **Budget in Vacation Time**—Just because you have started working for yourself, it doesn't mean that you should forfeit the fringe benefits that you deserve, including a well-earned vacation. Take the time to budget in vacation time. You may not be able to take concurrent weeks off, but there is a strong possibility that the vacation time can be parceled out and spread out over the year.

    Let's be honest: Burnout is real. It is also preventable. No matter how much you love what you do or how passionate you are, you need a break. By planning ahead of time, you can let your clients know or you can avoid scheduling any projects or events during your designated time away. One of the most rewarding aspects of earmarking vacation time is that you can include your family and friends in the process of both organizing and executing your plans.

The reality is that people do quit or suspend their freelancing careers because they can't find the sweet spot between what they may want to do and what they have to do. Just like in the game of tug-of-war, a 50/50 split may not be realistic. Yet, the interesting thing about being self-employed/freelancing is that our work/personal lives often intersect and they often overlap. The key is being clear about what work needs to looks like and what life needs to look like for you. And as much as I am speaking about this in generalized terms, your definition of balance is as unique as you are.

Seek Out Mentorship

Historically, in the Black community, elders are revered as the sages and history bearers. When growing up, I was strongly encouraged to sit at the feet of my elders and to just listen. This was often a difficult task for a little girl who was squirrely and adventurous.

Over time, I began to enjoy being around our church and neighborhood elders. In fact, I think I spent more time with older people than I did with my peers. This led to a profound respect and appreciation for listening to the life stories of people whose lived experiences were drastically different than my own. It also helped me to fully grasp that no matter what we do, we are never on this journey alone.

No one ever used the word mentorship to describe the relationships we were forging, but that's what it was. My mentors would take a keen interest in what we were doing and how we were doing it. If we were making mistakes or veering in the wrong direction, they would gently and sometimes firmly and caustically warn against our "making the same mistakes" that they did. They also served as sounding boards and griots whose stories were laden with lessons, words of wisdom and cautionary tales.

I was reminded of the importance of this recently as I had a chance to get away and be in the presence of women, who, like myself, have dedicated their careers to words, ideas, artistry and creativity. For almost four days, I was in a space where true mentorship not only mattered, it was centered and it was intentional. In some instances, I was mentoring others and in other moments, I was the mentee. At times, the line of demarcation was blurred. To say that it was magical was an understatement.

As I reflect back over this experience, I think about how and why mentorship is often undervalued; yet, it can have a profound effect on our growth and development as individuals and as entrepreneurs. Many of us would probably describe our experiences as ones that ebb and flow. Sometimes, it is during our growth spurts that we truly begin to embrace the value of having others on our journey with us. How often do we allow ourselves to say, "I don't know" or "I need help." How often is someone on the receiving side of those statements and ready to respond, "It is ok" or "Let me show you."

Both of these, in my estimation, are acts of courage, especially in a world where individuality is privileged and it is easier to pretend or go through the motions rather than taking off a mask and showing our vulnerabilities.

I had quite a few mask-removal moments this past weekend. Paradoxically, I was there because of a client who needed assistance with a writing project. I was there to work, but it is interesting how even work can become a space where we learn. I literally walked away rethinking how I approach my purpose for writing. It is my belief that the bonds that were formed that weekend will serve as anchors when the waters get rough and the horizon is too far to see.

Because the women I shared that space with truly did not want anything from me, I was able to give of myself in ways that I hadn't in a long time. It was liberating and humbling. They provided suggestions, feedback, guidance and words of encouragement. Isn't this what mentorship is all about?

We have a tendency to make mentorship convoluted and mechanical. We also seem to think that children or young adults are the only ones who need mentors—not true. When mentorship is born out of shared interests, it reflects a genuine desire to pull out the best in someone else. It is like making gumbo. You put together all of these ingredients that don't seem to go together to create the most delightful of tastes. Each ingredient pulls out the richness and flavor of the other ingredients. When you add intentionality and sincerity to the gumbo mix then mentorship really works.

Mentorship matters because so many of us work in isolation or we create in solitary ways. (I used to joke that my imaginary readers were becoming my closest friends). We must remind ourselves that even if others are not with us, we are not isolated and alone during this process. I often encounter others who have "left" freelancing because they felt so disconnected or did not see themselves as members of a community.

The truth is that being freelancers and entrepreneurs often means that many of us are not in spaces where people are readily available to mentor us. We may not even realize that we need mentoring. I have a business coach and I have a spiritual coach, but I did not think that I needed mentors until the moment when I knew that I needed mentoring.

It is for this reason that I encourage you to take time to reflect and to learn, but also to seek out people, locally or virtually, who will give you honest feedback and keep you inspired. If you feel like you don't need a mentor then become one.

Don't Talk to Strangers—Let's Rethink That

One of the greatest investments that I ever made was humbling myself enough to work with strangers on projects that we were all deeply vested in. In many ways, this goes against what we have been taught about competition in a free enterprise. However, I have found that collaboration with the right strangers can lead to amazing results.

How does it work?

Collaboration tools like Dropbox, secure FTP (file transfer protocol) and Google docs have made it a seamless process to work with strangers on a shared project. As with many work endeavors, there are often multiple layers and various components that individuals work on. With collaboration tools, some of those layers are peeled back as entrepreneurs literally become virtual co-workers with other entrepreneurs.

Having virtual co-workers means that you will probably also have to engage in virtual meetings and even webinars. Zoom, Skype, Google Hangout, Join Me, and other video hosting platforms have revolutionized the ways that some entrepreneurs organize and meet. Having virtual co-workers can lead to better communication protocols and clarity about the end goals. Information and content are shared, edited, curated, and co-created—often in real time.

Project management software like Podio and Basecamp have also made it easier for teams of entrepreneurs to work together. Couple that with the use of Office 360, Jostle, or Slack (cloud-based collaboration tools) and members of the team have access to a plethora of virtual resources and tools.

By default, we become members of shared virtual workspaces without leaving our homes or offices.

Examples of Projects
My first experience with working with virtual strangers was shortly after I left the classroom and I was serving as a contractor with a major publishing company. As the lead editor, I had team members who were, literally, all over the country. I quickly became immersed in the world of virtual curriculum writing which often requires people to work collaboratively with people whom they do not know and probably will never meet.

There was often a common blueprint—called specifications—that guided the process and a lead project manager who oversaw the entire team. Individual developers engaged in virtual conversations and team meetings without ever exchanging personal information. We would even have meetings where everyone was just a name or a voice.

I've also had a chance to work on grant projects with virtual strangers. Many smaller not-for-profit organizations may not have the resources that are necessary to contract with a professional grant writer or grant writing team. Therefore, they will often rely upon various individuals—some volunteer—to write sections of the narrative.

Many of these people may live in various parts of the country so the flexibility of being able to co-create is not only cost effective, but also efficacious. With some clarity and guidelines form the organizer, it's not only possible, but highly probable to create grants and other complex texts with strangers.

By engaging in a virtual space with virtual strangers, it allows for individuals to work on their sections of a project concurrently as opposed to having to wait for one person to finish a part of the project before someone else can work on it.

The Benefits
It's not uncommon to have some trepidation about sharing your ideas and work with others, but I have found that the long-term benefits of skills gained, resources generated, and relationships established far outweighed my initial concerns.

I do believe that some aspects of working with virtual strangers is going to be a significant part of the future of freelancing and gig economy jobs. As more corporations and private individuals are outsourcing their specific needs, it is highly likely that you will find yourself working with virtual co-workers. The more you understand about how it works, the better prepared you will be and the more competitive too!

My Takeaway
I highly recommend co-working with strangers. Of course, you want to be careful and treat it with the same business acumen as you would anything else (i.e. contract, payment information). Give it a chance if the opportunity presents itself. Although it's not applicable for all, sharing insight and collaborating with strangers can actually add value to your freelancing services and increase the types of services that you offer.

Your Time is an Investment in You

Time flies while you are having fun, or so they say. Well, actually, time is one of the greatest assets that you can have as a freelancer. But if you're not careful, it really can be easy to lose track of time or not account for your time wisely while you're engrossed in your work.

Thankfully, there are apps, devices, and techniques that you can use to improve your time management skills. The ones that I describe here are ones that I have used, but keep in mind that there are many others that may be just as beneficial to you throughout your freelancing endeavors.

Apps

Toggl: Each task that you complete takes a certain amount of time. If you have successfully completed versions of a task before, then you probably have a pretty clear sense of how long it will take you so you can plan accordingly. But let's say you have decided to take on a new project that takes you into unknown territory or that you have decided to work with a partner or on a team.

It's critically important that you manage the total amount of time that you spend on a project because time allocation can make the difference between realistic and unrealistic deadlines. For example, it may take you 3 hours to do something and you've only set aside 1 hour. Isolated, this may seem inconsequential, but if you multiply that by 5 to 6 projects then you have a real problem.

An app called Toggl is an excellent resource to determine exactly how long a project will take, but it's more than just a timer. As the name implies, you can toggle from task to task. There is also an analytic function that can be used to share data/results with others. Toggl not only helps you manage your individual time, but it keeps track of how long it takes the entire team to finish a task.

Devices

Phone Calendar Alerts: Are you overbooking or forgetting appointments? Even though missed appointments are often simple oversights, they don't bode well for sustaining and growing your clientele.

Smart phone calendar alerts can be a life saver when you are trying to manage your time. I admit that they can be annoying, but I am sure that many of us can attest to the fact that a calendar reminder made the difference between missing an event or making it.

Email calendars like Outlook and Google sync with smart devices, so gone are the days when you had to write down your appointments in multiple locations. For some of us, our phone is our virtual assistant and it helps us to not only organize, but to keep track of how we are spending our time.

A Dry Erase Board: Yes, this is old school, but there is something about seeing your own handwriting that gives a task great urgency and importance. So how will this help you manage your time? Well, things tend not to come off the dry erase board until they are completed.

If something remains on the board beyond its projected due date then that's a signal that you may want to rethink or reevaluate the amount of time that you are dedicating to that task. Conversely, are you spending too much time on another task?

Placement of the board is also important—don't hide it in an obscure room, put it somewhere where you have to see it and its contents. Psychologically, there's some built-in pressure to finish something that you can't ignore. [I have a portable one that goes with me and lives next to a dresser in my bedroom]. Lastly, there is that great satisfaction of erasing something on a board because it signals that you have successfully completed a task.

Techniques

Self-Progress Report: Although we may not have liked them, there was a reason why we received progress reports throughout our K-12 education. And in hindsight, they probably helped us, or our parents, monitor our academic progress. Well, progress reports can also be an asset when it comes to time management skills as an adult.

Here's what you can do: For one entire week, keep a journal or log of where you spend your time. Be honest and see this exercise as a self-assessment. After you have logged your time for a week, go back and look over the results. Ask: Where did I experience time misalignment?—or time spent doing things that were not a priority or not of importance (note, I intentionally did not use the word waste). After identifying where you spent your time, then shift and ask yourself why did I spend time engaging in that activity? Was it productive? Did I accomplish my end goal(s)?

If you take this report seriously, you will be amazed by what a week of self-reporting reveals about your current routine. Most importantly, you can use it to gauge whether or not you are using your time effectively. If not, develop a plan and execute it accordingly.

It is Ok to Slow Down

One day, I was playing around with the settings on my phone and I discovered that it tracked how much time I spent on Facebook—my favorite form of social media. I was shocked when I saw, in hours, my digital imprint on the outlet. I then juxtaposed those numbers with my project log and compared them both to the amount of time I spent actually doing things with friends and family members. It didn't look good.

Still curious, I started jotting down how much time I spent on the phone, watching TV, and running non-essential errands. Red flags emerged. Whereas I thought my 60-hour weeks were signs of my being a dedicated entrepreneur and being uber productive, this reality check proved otherwise.

Time for a Timeout

Being engrossed in a world measured by virtual steps and technological imprints had become so normal that I felt like a character in Ernest Cline's Ready Player One.

Over the course of three weeks, I intentionally made the decision to take an adult 'time out.' No FB (I even deleted the app), no TV (I removed it from my bedroom), only limited technology to honor client projects and other obligations. Whereas a time out may be seen as a form of punishment for young children, it actually proved to be quite rewarding. Paradoxically, by stepping away from the grind—as some people call it—I ended up being more productive.

We are Doing Too Much

My sister is an elementary school teacher and she has two expressions that I love. She'll say "they [my students] are doing too much" or "they are on a 10." Neither of these sentiments are exactly compliments. Let's just say she uses these expressions when her students are not on task and she needs to redirect them.

On the first day of my timeout, I thought a lot about how our culture just may be doing too much. We are in a historical moment where being too busy is seen as something good. The more you work, the better. The more you hustle, the better. The less you sleep, the better. The more you rely upon technology to function, the better.

With more time on my hands and less distractions, I actually started feeling like I was being too lazy or that my work ethic wasn't what it should be. I remember sitting and watching the snow fall one day. I literally felt anxious because I thought that I should be doing something. I had to recondition myself to understand that watching the snow fall, taking in its beauty, and just being still were actually doing something.

Rethinking Success
The person who is "so busy" and doesn't have time may realize that the time is there, it's just how we decide to use it. The key is being intentional and thoughtful. I cannot tell you how many times I wanted to cheat.

Seriously, look around us. On Instagram, I follow some diverse and interesting figures like P Diddy (I think he's going by that now) and Gary Vee. I am not going to lie, there have been times in the past when I feel like a complete failure because I could not function on 4 hours of sleep or I was incapable of recharging like the Energizer Bunny.

My point is that we've gotten to the point where we equate success, productivity, and even work ethic with being busy, but that's not necessarily true. You can be extremely busy and highly unproductive, as I discovered. My work week was not actually 60 hours—it never was—it just felt that way because I was always on the go.

By rethinking what I needed to do versus what I was doing, I actually accomplished more because I wasn't ripping and running for the sake of staying busy. Instead, I poured myself into things that were meaningful and valuable. I began to redefine my metrics for success and productivity by linking productivity to measurable end goals, including spending time meditating, in prayer, and journaling.

Being still, contemplative, and mindful led to more energy. Often, busyness is displaced energy. Sitting down, turning off a computer, tablet, or smart phone may seem counterproductive when your livelihood depends upon them, but having them on without a purpose is actually more problematic because we start to depend upon them to function. Worse yet, we think we might miss out on something important if we step back from the world. The reality, I found, is that we may be missing out on even more by not stepping back.

Stop to Smell the Roses
The energy and effort that we spend staying connected to technology can actually be re-purposed to spending time engaging with and creating real, not virtual, memories and emotional bonds with other people. I had no idea how many invites I had turned down, the infrequency in which I met with friends in real life, and the extent to which I was distancing myself from people who I truly loved and cared about.

For me, the end of my break was earlier this week and I don't think I can fully go back to the person who I was before. I do miss my Facebook community and I have started checking in and posting again. I lost a few friends during my hiatus and that's ok. I missed out on a few new TV series and that's ok as well.

I am more inclined now to reach out to friends to have lunch or do something sociable. I have also grown to enjoy sitting quietly and just listening. I don't see slowing down as being ineffective; I see it as a way to recharge, reboot and reposition myself to focus on the things that I value.

When I taught full-time, there would come a time during the semester when the push and pull of a full teaching load would take its toll. Mentally drained, physically tired, and emotionally spent, like clockwork, my body would tell me that I was in need of a time out. This would happen around December, just in time for winter break. After a few weeks off, I would often return refreshed, renewed, and reinvigorated to start a new semester.

As most of us know, breaks from freelancing don't quite work like that. Yes, we are prone to the same burnout or fatigue that others experience. And, yes, expending numerous intellectual, creative, and physical hours can lead to exhaustion. However, we often don't have the luxury of PTO (paid time off).

Does this mean that we should just suffer through? Absolutely not. Being the best freelancer possible requires being well-rested and giving oneself a chance to tune out the distractions and static that can drain us. It also means that we may need to plug into sources that recharge us and give us a renewed sense of purpose.

So, realistically, what does this look like? Here are three things that I love to do when freelancing fatigue kicks in. All of them are either reasonably priced or free.

Try a "staycation"
When is the last time that you explored your city? Have you ever decided to pretend to be a tourist and to go to some of the attractions that others visit when they come to your town? Better yet, when is the last time that you got out of the house and stayed in a local hotel? Staycations are an excellent way to check out without having to take on the added expense of travel.

Sites such as expedia.com, hotwire.com and travelocity.com make it relatively easy to book 3 to 4-star hotels at discounted rates. You can also avoid expensive hotel parking fees by taking Uber, Lyft, public transportation, or a cab. Wear some comfortable walking shoes and prepare to explore your city. Leave your laptop and other work-related gadgets at home. The point is for you to relax. If possible, splurge and take advantage of the hotels' amenities. Remember, you deserve it!

Get outside

We are entering into that time of the year when the weather is (slightly) more predictable and you don't have to wear a bulky coat to venture out. National parks can be amazing, but don't overlook the jewels that just may be in your own backyard. You don't have to hop on a plane to take full advantage of this relaxing activity. In other words, have you thought about visiting a local or state park?

Many of these parks have minimal entry fees and they have observatories, natural trails and hiking paths that make for an excellent full-day's agenda. Rich with both physical activities and opportunities to be mindful and to reflect, hiking and walking are great ways to take your mind off of work. Take a book or take a journal to write and to unwind, but do not take work-related projects. Put your phone on vibrate or silent and focus on the awesomeness of your surroundings. Let nature recharge you.

Volunteer

My company did a day of service at a local transitional housing facility; we also did a book drive and we are planning more events. We are going back to do a cover letter-writing and resume-writing workshop for the residents. The key to engaging in successful volunteer opportunities is to think about your skillset, gifts, and talents and to find organizations that are a good match. Volunteering is an excellent way to share your gifts with the community.

Ask yourself: Are there organizations in my city that could benefit from what I have to offer in-kind? Whether it is a one-time volunteer event or a long-term relationship, giving back is an excellent way to not only help but to engage in something that is bigger than you—being of service to others and being connected to members of your community.

When you find yourself on empty and you need to refuel, try one of these strategies. The key to dealing with burnout or fatigue is recognizing when it's coming on. Perhaps you are feeling irritable or you are short tempered or you are not as motivated or inspired as you typically are. It is ok—it's just your body's way of telling you that you need to slow down and take a break.

With some planning and consideration, taking a few hours or even a day or two to step away from the desk can actually be incredibly rewarding. The reality is that you have earned it, so make sure that you are taking the time to get the rest, relaxation, and reconnection that you need.

Throughout this Journey, You will Need More than Motivation—You will Need Opportunities

Every week, I come across publications, outlets and individuals who are seeking freelance or contract writers. Some want people with extensive portfolios, while others are not concerned about experience or pedigree. As I have perused these various calls for writers (and as I have experienced in my own writing career), there are certain things that freelance writers, in particular, can do to position themselves for sustainable writing careers. If you are not a writer, think about how you can apply these tips to your industry.

Diversify your areas of expertise
If you really want a chance to bring in enough income to sustain writing full-time, I strongly recommend that you don't become fixated on one area of specialization or niche audience. Recently, I have seen paid writing gigs for fashion writers, medical writers, news writers, travel writers, sports writers, and everything in between.

In previous careers, many of us may have been trained to specialize to the point of exclusivity. In the world of freelance writing, this can backfire. There is nothing wrong with being a subject matter expert, but you have to honestly ask yourself: Is there enough demand for content about my area of expertise that it will sustain me?

Sustain a virtual presence
When I first started blogging, I wrote almost exclusively about education and diversity issues. Although I was vested in these topics and deeply passionate about them, I was pigeonholing myself. After a while, I became known as "the education writer." I had so much more to offer and write about, but it was not reflected in my work. To change this, I started writing about other topics, and now my writing portfolio reflects a diverse range of interests and audiences.

As a result, my writing has helped me to maintain a virtual presence and to sustain a tangible digital imprint.

Consider alternative opportunities

There are colleges and universities that offer degrees in technical writing, but I am not suggesting that you go back to school. Instead, I am recommending that you don't sweep aside writing opportunities that are more technical in nature, like manual writing or curriculum writing.

Yes, these may not be as interesting as writing full-length articles or shorter blogs, but they do pay well and once you have a track record for writing them, it becomes easier to navigate the jargon and buzzwords that often accompany these types of writing opportunities. To get a sense of the scope of freelance and contract technical writing jobs, you may want to start with: www.indeed.com (use technical writing as your search term).

Share your work

Sharing is caring, and this is especially true when it comes to establishing and sustaining a freelance writing career. It may sound self-serving, but you need to be your biggest cheerleader. Whether it's via social media, email, text, or causal conversation, tell people about your written work. You will be amazed by how people will start to think of you as "the writer." This, in turn, can lead to unsolicited opportunities to write and to get paid to do so.

In addition, sharing your work helps prime you for receiving feedback—both constructive and intrusive. If you are going to sustain a freelance writing career, you cannot have a thin skin. The sooner you acclimate to hearing positive and negative feedback, the more comfortable you will become. You also want to brace yourself for rejection. Early on, my work was rejected more times than it was accepted; of course, this was difficult to accept, but it also motivated me to become a more thoughtful writer.

Read more

This one may seem odd. What in the world does reading have to do with freelance writing? Well, reading diverse content can help freelance writers not only study the skill of writing, but process the mechanics of it as well.

Reading can better position you to understand how you write and how writing for an audience—both real and imagined—affects your craft. Unlike writing exclusively for oneself, paid freelance writing is always geared towards an audience. Being keenly aware of how your readers may potentially interact or interface with your words is critical in how you approach the task of writing for others.

Be adventurous and read outside of your comfort zone. If you like James Joyce's writing style, try Ernest Hemingway's. In other words, if you tend to gravitate towards a particular writing style, switch it up and try another one, just to see what it feels like from a reader's standpoint. The more you can pinpoint what good writing looks and feels like, the more you will be able to develop your own style and connect with an audience.

Lean into discomfort
For me, sustainability is the key to a fruitful and rewarding career. Freelance writing can be an enjoyable experience, especially when you are able to write about topics that you are knowledgeable of and/or passionate about. But, it can also be equally as powerful when you have to lean into discomfort or stretch to write about topics that are new to you.

Budget and Plan for Professional and Personal Development

Creating a budget for your freelancing services is by far one of the greatest assets that you can have. Budgets provide us with visual reminders of our projected income, shortfalls, and overall expenditures. Budgeting is also an opportunity to establish priorities as to where and how you want to use your resources.

Standard line items like supplies, office space (if applicable), contractor fees, and utilities such as WIFI and cell phone bills often make their way to budgets, because these expenses tend to be universal for many of us. But, there is another line item that some of us may not have thought about that can have a tremendous impact on our growth and development as entrepreneurs —professional development or PD.

What is professional development?
I first became familiar with PD as a graduate student. We could apply for funding to attend conferences, workshops, and/or lectures that were related to our field of study or discipline. As the name implies, professional development revolves around learning new trends, best practices, and ongoing developments in one's field.

Businessdictionary.com defines professional development as the "process of improving and increasing capabilities of staff through access to education and training opportunities in the workplace through outside organization, or through watching others perform the job. Professional development helps build and maintain morale of staff members and is thought to attract quality staff to an organization."

In an entrepreneurial capacity, think about PD as a chance to take a deep dive into a topic or area of interest that will better position you to do your job. Because we often work in isolation, we may not always be aware of significant changes—the types of changes that can prove to be advantageous.

Why is professional development beneficial to entrepreneurs? Although self-imposed PD may not have the formality or the same requirements as the continuing education units (CEU)/credits or the recertification process that is required by some disciplines, it can have a profound impact on how well a freelancer is able to maintain their professional standing amongst their peers and clients.

PD keeps entrepreneurs up-to-date about changes such as any new rules, new software, improved resources, and changing compensation guidelines. Experts or Subject Matter Experts (SMEs) are often brought in to share their stories and real-world strategies that have benefitted them and can potentially benefit others. Depending on the nature of the PD, entrepreneurs may also have the opportunity to buy resources like books, CDs, DVDs, and curricula.

From editors and accountants to registered dietitians and legal counselors, there are myriad chances to seek out and take advantage of professional development opportunities. In addition, PD, whether via webinars or live conferences, provides entrepreneurs with an opportunity to connect and network with other entrepreneurs. These informal connections are not only beneficial from a professional context, but they also create opportunities to build relationships and bonds with other entrepreneurs who have similar interests.

How much should you budget?

Most national organizations and associations have annual conferences that are planned at least a year in advance. With the shifting economy, many of these organizations now recognize that their members and conference participants are not necessarily anchored to institutions. As such, there is often the option to register as an independent participant. And sometimes the registration fee is slightly lower for those who are self-employed, especially since the fees of many of the other participants will be absorbed by larger corporations and institutions.

With the host city, hotel fees, and registration costs often listed publicly on websites, it is possible to project and plan ahead well in advance. Once a per diem for food, travel cost like airfare, and other miscellaneous costs are factored in, it is possible to create a realistic budget for PD.

Carving out your budget for PD should revolve around picking the options that are going to give you the greatest bang for your buck. Each year, consider incrementally increasing your PD budget. Of course, it is great if more than one PD opportunity is fiscally feasible for you. After attending a few, it should become clear why this line item is worth it.

4

TECHNIQUES FOR DEVELOPING YOUR IDEA

Art is the chalice into which we pour the wine of transcendence.

-Stanley Kunitz

Now that you have identified your idea and we have explored why it is important to invest in yourself, it is time to discuss the technical side of your gift or your specific skill set. If you think of your gift as something that comes naturally to you then your skill set revolves around how you monetize that gift. In other words, just because someone has the gift of writing doesn't mean that the person sees him/herself as a professional writer.

Thus, one of the mistakes that aspiring entrepreneurs will make is that they do not clearly articulate or carve out their skill set before they launch. It all begins with answering this question: What can I do so well that people will compensate me to do it?

In answering this question, it is not uncommon to hit a wall. And it is not uncommon for fear and a lack of confidence to seep in.

This metaphoric wall can be the result of underdeveloped ideas, lack of motivation, distractions, lack of clarity, and/or life. It is the last one that gets most of us.

Blockage is enough to make the most seasoned person take a time out and even contemplate quitting. Unfortunately, there is no way to forecast exactly when it is going to happen, but it happens.

The key, paradoxically, is not attempting to avoid it, but coming up with coping strategies to help you deal with it when it does occur. In other words, we have to do our best to prepare ourselves to push through and to write on.

Too often, as writers in particular, we meander as we try to get our words out of our heads and on to a sheet of paper. Wouldn't life just be easier if we could skip that step and our readers could meet us at the genesis of our ideas and simply understand everything that we are trying to say?

Of course that's not plausible, so it's up to us to make sure that we are clear in our expression of thought. For some, that can lead to anxiety, angst, fear, and blockage.

Telling a writer to 'just calm down' or 'get over it' are not helpful—at all. These sentiments, instead, do more harm than good as they don't really acknowledge that writing can be incredibly difficult and even painful, even for skilled writers.

So, what can a writer do? In fact, what can any of us do?

Unfortunately, some of us sacrifice our well-being and are in perpetual hamster-on-a-wheel mode. We are moving, but we aren't going anywhere.

When this happens, ask yourself: When is the last time that I did something for me? Not my career, not my family, not my friends, and not my community, but simply for me because I deserve it.

If it helps, start keeping a journal of how many hours a week you spend writing versus other things. How many of those hours are dedicated for writing? Do you have 5 hours to yourself and you spend 3 minutes of those hours writing? This may seem like a hyperbole, but until you actually track where you spend your time, you just might be amazed by where you are NOT spending your time.

One of my sister's favorite expressions is, "You are doing too much." And perhaps, you are. As I noted in a previous chapter: It is possible that your writer's block is connected to stress. Try de-stressing and see if that opens up a space for your creative and intellectual energies to flow.

For many professional writers, we are goal-driven overachievers who have found a way to convert our skills, talents, and gifts into profitable enterprises. The thought of slowing down or stopping may seem oxymoronic, but it is necessary.

I find that burnout often occurs when we don't have the stamina to keep up at our current pace or we are engaging in practices that are not sustainable. Let's be honest, operating on 3 to 4 hours of sleep is not optimal, yet some of us do it on a daily basis. And then we get up expecting to just chisel away at the keyboard—is that realistic?

My number one antidote to writer's block is self-care. Take the time to do things that refuel you.

When my soul is fed, I write. In fact, I write a lot. While coaching clients, I find that the key is being proactive and not reactionary to the demands of writing. Once you sense that you are losing vigor, it's time to rethink your action plan.

I do three things that have worked quite well:

1. Step back
2. Reevaluate
3. Reprioritize

In other words, tackle the things that are most time sensitive and urgent then make a plan for everything else, keeping in mind that you need to set aside some time for you. If it is appropriate and the project calls for it, lean on others to help you with it or see if someone in your support system can help you with your other responsibilities so that you can just write.

Writing is often a solitary act and many writers tend to forget that your words are an extension of you, so when you are your best self, it positions you to do your best work.

Is Going Back to School Necessary?

Any discussion about skills inevitably leads to a discussion about formal education. This is particularly true for those of you who may be shifting from one industry to one that is totally different. This may lead to the question of: Is going back to "school" necessary? (I have intentionally placed school in question marks because it has become such a nebulous concept since the time when, if you are old enough to remember, all schooling implied a brick and mortar building.)

With businesses like graphic design, photography, event planning, and even writing, does one really need a degree to get ahead professionally?

This is not an easy question to answer. I come from a family where a college education was of the utmost importance. It wasn't if we were going to college, it was where we were going to college. Mandatory college attendance was drilled into me since I was little girl. I never questioned it and it became a normal part of my life's trajectory because I lived in a world of binaries: People who attended college had the best jobs, lived in the nicest neighborhoods and drove luxury, foreign cars. People who didn't attend college struggled. Albeit flawed, it was a simple equation.

Looking back, I know this worldview was extreme. Life has definitely shown me that a college degree is not a guarantee of financial or material success.

The New Work Economy
The reality is that times have changed drastically since I was a little girl. Data reveals that skills-based gig economies are shifting the

narrative of what it means to be prepared for a good job. A recent article in MIC states:

"As of 2015, 54 million people were working as freelancers or independent contractors, and they're estimated to earn 17% more per hour than traditional employees. It's even projected that 60% of companies plan to hire more freelancers than full-time employees, with 45% expecting to increase hiring of freelancers by 30% or more by 2020. As the gig economy expands in America and emphasis on adaptability widens, higher learning is now being reimagined to draw on hands-on work experience and specific skill sets."

As the economy shifts, so must the way that we prepare and train workers. With entrepreneurship and gig economies becoming more readily accessible and commonplace, it's time that we have a conversation about how freelancing is altering the way that we think about education, especially traditional college programs.

Skills over Degrees?
I have drawn the conclusion that we may need to place greater emphasis on skills than degrees when we think about the steps that are needed to establish and secure a sustainable career. Let's be honest—college is not for everyone and not all professions require a formal education.

To be fair, I am not painting with too broad of a stroke because certain independent contractors and entrepreneurs must have college degrees or terminal degrees in order to practice in their fields. Yet in other industries one can be self-taught, and experiential knowledge is seen as equally as valuable, if not more valuable, than textbook knowledge.

So, this is not a one size fits all conversation. However, I do think the real solution can be found in having meaningful conversations about what hands-on experience actually looks like and where it can be gained.

Solutions: A Hybrid Approach
After going through hundreds of resumes looking for freelance

writers for a large, multiple-month project, I noticed that many of the applicants had the technical knowledge, but not the pragmatic experience.

When I asked for published writing samples, my candidate pool shrunk tremendously. The problem wasn't ability, it was experience. (Based on the Word documents that they sent, many of them could write well, but my client was particular in that she only wanted people on the team who had experience writing for national audiences.)

So, I decided to do something about it. I created an internship program for Seldon Writing Group, LLC. The internship is designed so that knowledge-based learning and skills-based learning are mutually inclusive.

After a vetting process, I have welcomed two millennial interns. They both have English degrees from well-established universities and well-paying full-time jobs. So, why in the world would they take on the extra work and time commitment of interning as adults? Because they realized that learning didn't end when they walked across the stage.

We focus on one skill at a time (e.g. blogging, editing, ghost writing) until they have gained proficiency. I review their work and give them comprehensive feedback. I walk them through where to find freelance job leads and how to apply.

There is no online course, no set hours per week, and no certification process, just some good old-fashioned hard work. They gain demonstrable real-world skills that they can leverage to get paid writing gigs. In turn, I've helped to train a new cohort of freelance writers. It is a win-win.

Most importantly, they are gaining some pragmatic skills that they did not receive during their tenure as college students. Neither of them regrets their college experiences. They just thought, like many of us, that a college degree would be like a magic wand that opens doors and creates opportunities. They now realize that it takes more and it's for this reason that we need to be serious about the impactfulness of entrepreneurship, which takes me back to the title of this vignette.

But that still may not satisfactorily answer the question that this chapter poses. In concrete terms, "No. Going back to school is not necessary." Some parents and some of my former colleagues in academia may be surprised by this answer. But here's why:

Since transitioning into freelancing, I have uncovered an entire ecosystem where one's degree or where one obtained it from is more of an ancillary conversation than a pre-requisite for employment. What seems to be most important is: Can you do the work? Are your skill sets comparable with the need or demand?

Because of this, it is time that we rethink the "college or else" mentality. It puts a lot of unnecessary pressure on people who may not need to go that route in order to be successful. And it's not fair to those who attend just to discover that they are unprepared for what they really want to do in life.

Obtaining a college degree should be a personal decision, but it's equally as important that people know that they have options and that one can be successful with or without a degree.

If nothing else, freelancing has definitely taught me that there are many things that simply cannot be taught in a classroom or gleaned from a book. Even in my mid-40s, I am still learning and it has nothing to do with the spoonful of alphabet soup behind my name.

Content is King and Queen

You may be thinking that this section only applies to those of you who are writers—not quite.

What "location location, location" is to real estate, "content, content, content" is to entrepreneurship, regardless of industry.

Whether you are new or a pro, content drives what you do, the frequency in which you do it, and the likelihood of your writing leading to the desired results (to inform, persuade, educate, etc.).

Yet, content generation can be one of the most difficult things about blogging. How do you come up with meta ideas? How do you know if an audience will vibe with your content? How do you produce original content?

These questions often swirled around in my head when I first started, but as I transitioned from sticking my big toe in the water to diving right in, I learned that when it comes to content development, you are in control and it's not as daunting as it may seem and here's why:

Read
I am a reader by nature, but once I started blogging, I shifted from being a reader to being a reading scout. Just as NBA scouts will study potential college players to determine if they are a 'fit', a reading scout will peruse the internet and print outlets looking for great stories and topics to explore. I often find that some of my topic ideas are the direct result of something that piqued my interest even if my original intent was not to write about that subject.

I keep a folder titled "Use Later" and it's filled with various topics that I have uncovered while scouting. Because I write for different outlets, the folder is comprised of a myriad of incongruent topics that I can draw from when, or if, I need to—hence, it is a savings account.

Evergreen Content
Another big mistake that I made when I first started blogging was writing, almost exclusively, about current events. Something interesting would happen in the news and I would try to get a blog post out that same day or the next day at the latest. This proved to be taxing and writing started to feel more like a chore than something I thoroughly enjoyed.

I realized that the urgency and interest in current event blogs often dissipated within hours of my uploading them. So I started to focus more on what some bloggers call evergreen topics—or topics that are timeless. These topics are still viable months and even years after they are written.

For example, two years ago, I wrote a blog about how WWI served as a political springboard for the Harlem Renaissance. The blog was written for informative purposes, and although it was about a specific historic moment, the facts are immutable. I just reposted the blog on social media last month. And I will probably share it again on social media in a few months. Why? Because the content is still relevant even though I did not write it recently.

In essence, evergreen content can be ageless; as such, a blogger can get more traction out of it, especially when sharing it on various social media platforms.

This does not mean that current events should be off limits for content generation; instead, I recommend that you focus on a nice balance between the two depending on who you are writing for and why.

Pick Interesting Titles and Pictures
When we think about blog content, we may only think about the written text, but that's a misstep. The title of your blog and the picture will probably be two of the first things that potential readers encounter. In fact, they may be the determining factors if someone will even click the link to read your content.

Because these two carry so much weight, it is tempting to engage in what is called 'click-bait' where the heading and even the picture are intentionally misleading, salacious, and/or controversial because they will seduce the reader into clicking the link, only for him/her to find out that the actual written content is about something else or that it is not aligned to the title.

I strongly recommend that you do not sacrifice quality or your ethical responsibility to the reader just to get reads. Instead, pick titles that capture what the blog is about. A thoughtful and informed reader will decide if they want to read further.

Lastly, if you plan to blog frequently and you have editorial control over the images, it may be worth your while to purchase a membership to a stock image platform.

If you are committed to launching a career as a blogger (or writer), make sure that once you have a firm grasp on how to generate and maintain your content, you engage in another c word that is equally as important and that's consistency.

Value You: Pricing Out Your Services

"How much should I charge for my goods or services?"

It is, by far, one of the questions that I hear the most often. As an entrepreneur, it's important that you are intentional and thoughtful about your prices. But how you set them is up to you. Should you charge a flat rate, by the project, by the hour or some hybrid rate for your services?

Although this section is written with writers in mind, it will explore some popular pricing methods that can be used in other fields and industries.

By the Word
With software like Microsoft and the ability to do an accurate word count, charging by the word is pretty straightforward regardless of the size of the document.

However, there is a slight caveat that I learned along the way. If you charge by the word, you may want to think about word ranges, instead of an exact number. For example, if you have been asked to write a blog for a client and your fee is .10 a word, you don't want to get to the 500th word and just stop. So, by pricing it out as a 500 to 600-word blog post, it gives you some cushion. Furthermore, the client will know that a blog post of that length will range from $50 to $60 depending on the final word count.

There is an elephant in the room when it comes to charging by the word and it's one that I didn't anticipate: Are articles words? I had a client who did not consider articles like a, an, and the words. So, I had to factor those out when I did the final invoicing. It was a fairly long project and going through and making sure that I did not include them was painstaking. [I suspect there is some software out there that can do this, but I was unaware of it].

My takeaway for anyone who opts to use this pricing method is to be clear about what constitutes a word as it relates to your pricing.

By the Hour
By the hour is still one of the more difficult pricing methods for me. I have worked on some projects enough that I know exactly how long it will take me; however, others are a guessing game. For example, if I'm writing an 800-word blog post about a topic that I'm familiar with and it does not require additional research, I know that I can write it in about an hour. If my hourly rate is $85.00 then I would charge a rate of $85.00 for that blog post.

However, if I've been commissioned to write a post about a topic that I'm unfamiliar with and it requires me to read additional articles in order to familiarize myself with the material then that same 800-word post may now take 3 hours to complete when I factor in the time that it takes to conduct research. In turn, if I charge by the hour, it will now cost my client $255.00 for my services. Some clients will understand this and others may find that price to be too lofty.

Another issue I've encountered is underestimating or overestimating how much time it's going to take you from start to finish, which means that you may either undercharge or overcharge your clients. If you do opt to charge by the hour, be mindful that if it does take you longer than you initially told your client, then you will have to take the hit.

Conversely, if it takes you less time, are you willing to offer a refund? For these reasons, honestly, I avoid charging by the hour.

By the Page
By the page is another method that you may want to consider. Before you start, I recommend that you first determine what constitutes a page: Is it double or single spaced? 12 or 14 pt. font? Does 3/4 of a page count? What about a quarter of a page? These may seem like inconsequential questions, but believe it or not, the inability to make

this clear from the beginning can make a measurable difference in terms of your productivity and overall profitability.

The good news is that most clients have a sense of the total number of pages that they want you to write. Like writing by the word, I recommend that you do a page range +/- 5 to 10 pages depending on the project, so that you have some additional wiggle room if those extra pages help you to convey your ideas more effectively. Of all of the services that I offer, this one seems to work the best with ghostwriting.

By the Project
As I have matured as a freelance writer and gained more experience with some of the previously mentioned forms of pricing, I've learned over the years that by the project is my favorite pricing method. Most of my clients already have a budget in mind. If I think the project amount is fair and reasonable, I will accept the pricing as is.

If, based on my prior knowledge, I anticipate that the client's compensation for the project is unrealistic, I may re-negotiate—keep in mind that if you try this approach, you need to be in a position to explain why. In other instances, saying "no thank you" is also a viable option, especially if the client's suggested compensation is not within your typical range and he/she is not in position to alter the amount.

What's Best for You?
There is no 'one size fits all'. I have tried all of these and it truly was trial and error that led me to gravitate towards by the page and by the project while avoiding by the hour.

The most important thing is that whether you use one pricing method or a combination, keep in mind that you want to be fairly compensated and transparent with your clients.

As You Build Your Clientele, Don't Overlook This

Even with the advancement of social media, digital marketing, robo-emails, and other automated options that make building one's clientele roster more efficient, there is still something endearing about good old-fashioned word of mouth. Not only is it free, but it typically is embedded in and built upon trust.

Yet, as easy and as simplistic as that may sound, what makes word of mouth work is that it is organic. There is no algorithm, but there are some things that you can do to help your clients have an exceptional experience.

Customer Service, Customer Service, Customer Service

I remember one time when I was searching for a car. I loved a specific European brand, make, and model so I narrowed my choice to a particular dealership. I went in several times and the sales staff overwhelmed me with attention, reading materials, and all the espresso that one could drink.

They used terms like 'family' and 'valued' customer. I was assigned a personal sales agent who picked me up from work one day so that I could test drive the car. He kept telling me to "take the corners," so I did. It was exhilarating. Needless to say, the amazing customer service wowed me and it was a deciding factor in my purchasing the car.

A few days after picking up the car, I had a question and could not find the answer in the elaborate, but not-so-user friendly, car book. When I called to speak to my sales agent, he immediately replied, "Tyra who?" I thought: *How many Tyras have you sold cars to in the last 3 days?*

Gone was the overly effervescent personality and *we are family* mantra. His voice didn't even sound the same. And even after I jogged his memory as to who I was, he was indifferent and he could not answer my question.

When I asked to speak to the director of sales, I was told that he would call me back at his earliest convivence. This was in 2002; it is 2019 and I am still waiting for that return phone call. And no, I never found out the answer to my question. To borrow from a phrase that was popular in the 90s and 00s, I got played.

Service after the sale, in this capacity, required engaging with the customer. Although I do not recall my exact question, a return phone call or even a: "We don't know" would have gone a long way to rebuilding my trust and respect for this business.

Why Word of Mouth Really Matters
Later, when several of my colleagues or friends asked about my car, I told them that I would drive to Philly or Baltimore before I ever purchased another car from that dealership or recommended them to someone else. I tried to remain diplomatic—perhaps my experience was an outlier, but what if it wasn't?

I did not want to run the risk that people who I respected and cared about might have a similar experience. If they thought enough of my opinion to ask for it, I wanted to be fair and honest.

Like most friendships, familial or even work relationships, we all have a sphere of influence and that is why word of mouth is critical. Word of mouth is a pseudo-vetting process that some potential clients depend upon when determining who they want to work with. And, based upon the relationship between the parties involved, one person's endorsement can carry quite a bit of weight.

The poor customer service that I experienced left such a sour taste in my mouth that I will never forget that experience, but for all of the wrong reasons. Conversely, I have had amazing experiences where the business' representatives were attentive and responsive. On numerous occasions, I have referred other people to these businesses.

Clearly, we want our clients to remember us; we want our clients to have an exceptional experience and when they do, there is a stronger likelihood that they will, via word of mouth, make referrals. And because word of mouth is still one of the best ways to gain new clientele, be sure to make customer service a priority in how you deal with clients—before, during, and after the sale.

Tyra L. Seldon, Ph.D.

Crowdfunding As a Means to Fund Your Idea

When you first ventured into the world of freelancing, you may have used a funding source commonly referred to as "bootstrapping." This simply means that you used your own money to cover your start-up costs. Others have relied on investors or personal loans and some have leveraged capital from family and friends to jump start their freelancing careers.

Thankfully, for those who may not have or cannot save up enough money or who don't have access to traditional funding streams, there is another form of funding that is a great fit for entrepreneurs. Crowdfunding has become a popular way for some entrepreneurs, small business owners, and entrepreneurs to raise initial funding and/or to accelerate their businesses.

When I learned about crowdfunding a few years ago, I was hesitant because I have this thing about asking people for money, but my views have changed drastically as I have watched other people launch successful crowdfunding campaigns that yielded great results. Here are some examples of some of the most successful campaigns:

What do successful campaigns have in common?

Have a good story
One of the most obvious is a backstory or captivating narrative for why a person is seeking funding and why his/her project/business is needed. The story often takes on the same characteristics of any good, persuasive writing.

Since you are asking people for something, it makes sense that you must convince them why they should believe you. To be honest, you have to be clear about what they will get out of it. Paradoxically, even though you are the one raising the funds, it is not about you; instead, it is about why others should invest in your vision, your idea, your business or your dream. Make sure that your pitch is engaging, lucid, and compelling.

Use the right platform
It is not enough to just have a good story. Also make sure that you are using a crowdfunding platform that is a good fit for your freelancing goals.

There are two types of platforms: rewards-based and equity crowdfunding. Rewards-based platforms like kickstarter.com and indiegogo.com allow people to donate without having equity in your project/business—keep in mind that some campaigns are all or nothing, so be realistic about your funding goals. It is also worth noting that these platforms have fees associated with them.

Another option is equity crowdfunding, which allows people to become actual shareholders in your company. This platform may be optimal for those entrepreneurs who want to launch businesses. Two platforms that you might want to consider are crowdfunder.com and circleup.com. Indiegogo recently added the option of equity crowdfunding on their platform as well. As with anything, make sure that you read all of the fine print and that you are comfortable with the platform, its services, and the fees.

Marketing, marketing, marketing
This last step is the one that I struggle with the most—marketing. Poor marketing can ruin even the best business endeavors. This is why marketing is critical to every crowdfunding campaign. How do you gather a crowd or let people know that you are raising money?

Most of us will start with the familiar—friends and family.

I love my friends and family, but if you rely exclusively on them then there is a strong possibility that you are not casting a wide enough net. Instead, leverage your existing network that includes family, friends, former clients, current clients, school alums (e.g. high school, college), groups that you belong to, and lastly, members of your social media family. But don't just post it and leave it—actively engage people by asking them to share it within their networks.

Another technique that seems to work is "bartering" with someone who has a larger network. I may have 1,000 friends/followers/connections and someone else may have 100,000. A simple shout out from the person with the larger platform and a link to the campaign will suffice. Also, think about doing FB live, Snapchat and/or Periscope videos.

If you are not a fan of social media, you can write guest blogs and include information about the campaign; you can also appear on traditional radio shows and/or podcasts that reach your targeted audience. The key is driving visitors to your crowdfunding landing page.

A good crowdfunding campaign is only as good as the traffic that it generates. Once people get to the campaign, your content should help convert a visit into a DONATE.

EXECUTION

5

LEVERAGING YOUR CREDENTIALS, PRIOR KNOWLEDGE AND LIFE EXPERIENCES

If you think you can do a thing or think you can't do a thing, you're right.

-Henry Ford

As you get acclimated to the concept of fully executing your idea, you will want to start thinking about growth. At some point during your entrepreneur life, you may have thought about scaling up or going from being an independent contractor to an actual business. This is not a minor decision as it has implications for other variables in your life, including marketing, revenue, and taxes.

As someone who used her freelancing skills as a springboard to start a business, I thought that it might be helpful to ask you a few practical questions. The answers of which may save you some headaches, sleepless nights, and unwarranted stress. As with anything that involves your time, talent, and resources, I recommend that you look at this through various lenses to determine if any, or all, of it applies to you.

So, what do you need to consider before leveraging your freelancing career to launch a business?

Am I legally a business? This is, by far, is one of the most important questions that you need to ask yourself. My decision to create a business was determined by the mission and vision that I had for my company. Once I personally navigated the world of 1099s, I started envisioning having a company with employees. I wanted to eventually bring on board other freelancers so that I could increase my volume and go after larger contracts. I met with several people who owned businesses to determine if an LLC, Inc, or S Corp was the best option for me.

Based on tax shelters, my industry, and future earning potential and projections, I decided that an LLC (limited liability company) was the most viable option. With an LLC, the members of the company are not personally liable for the company's liabilities or debts. I researched what my state required—keep in mind that every state is different—thankfully, the process was straightforward so I was able to file all of the necessary paperwork myself. Others have told me that some states are far more complicated and they have hired others to do the paperwork for them.

Obviously, there is not 'one size fits all', so be sure to do your research on the front end.

Am I ready, financially and otherwise to deal with liability issues? There are several wonderful things about owning a company, but there are also responsibilities or potential liabilities that you will take on. To be honest, you don't want to position yourself to be the subject of someone else's scorn or lawsuit. In this light, your status as a company offers you some protection as an individual that being a freelancer does not.

Also related to liability is acquiring an EIN (federal employer identification number). It is a unique nine-digit number that you can apply for via the IRS website. In a nutshell, the EIN is like your company's social security number. It is primarily used for identification purposes, but it is also highly beneficial for other reasons. You can use your EIN to open a business bank account, acquire business credit, secure additional funding, and pay your independent contractors. Go to www.irs.gov and follow the instructions for applying for an LLC.

Do you have the infrastructure in place to help you as you grow? If there are two services that you don't want to skim on, it's your legal and accounting services. I recommend retaining a CPA because as you scale up, your expenses will increase as will your paperwork and your need to save and systemize your accounting practices.

It's also definitely worth your while to invest in a lawyer. Before seeking out legal counsel, uncover as much information as possible to determine what your state's laws are and how they will affect you if you formalize your business. Doing your homework will help a lawyer advise you. Lawyers are also great resources when you are either generating or entering into contracts.

Some business owners will opt to pay their accountants and lawyers a monthly retainer, while others will use a fee for service payment method. Regardless of which method you use, you need to be prepared for the extra overhead costs that you will have. Obviously, there will be some additional costs involved with shifting from being a freelancer to a business, but these two are definitely non-negotiables.

Lastly, I would recommend that you think about where you want to be 3 to 5 years from now. This will help you to determine if you are in step to making those goals a reality. If becoming a business is your pathway to success then I highly recommend that you consider doing it.

Also, keep in mind that I know of several people who are gainfully employed who have not formalized their services. They have opted to maintain their status as self-employed or sole proprietor because it's not beneficial for them to do otherwise. So, in a nutshell, this really is a personal choice.

You are Neither Too Young Nor Too Old to Execute Your Idea

I once wrote a blog about the lessons that I have learned as a freelancer in her 40s. The blog was my attempt to encourage others to think about the viability of freelancing later in life. Little did I know that it would strike such a chord, and even a nerve, with so many people.

Some commenters questioned why including my age was such an important part of my narrative. Others suggested that being older was a disadvantage and yet others shared stories of how they had experienced discriminatory practices and implicit biases from others.

Interestingly, as I read the comments and considered their implications, I thought about how age is a topic that we don't often talk about. And when we do talk about age, the conversation tends to ducktail many of the negative things that go along with it. We seem to be more comfortable talking about race, gender, sexuality, and even socio-economic class.

The reality is that no one can wake up in the morning and say, now which of these identities will I put on or take off today? In the ubiquitous words of the woman from the TV commercial, "That's not how it works; that's not how any of this works."

When it comes to the time for you to fully execute your business, be mindful that it will not happen at the same time for you that it does for everyone else. I have clients who launched in their 20s and I have another client in her 60s who plans to launch. In other words, who you are and what you bring to this stage is going to be determined by your life experiences, your worldview, and your prior knowledge. These things, as I will discuss shortly, are actually advantageous when it comes to executing your ideas.

The intersections of our identities are what make each of us whole, unique individuals. Kimberle Crenshaw, Professor of Law at UCLA, first coined the term intersectionality as a way to help us to understand the interconnected nature of categories such as race, class, age, and gender. These categories overlap and seep into our professional and personal lives.

Intersectionality grapples with the multiple avenues through which oppression can be experienced and how certain members of a group can experience erasure simply by also being part of another group.

Intersectionality is critically important for freelancers and creative entrepreneurs because as we engage in our crafts, we do so as individuals with varied and diverse life experiences who are also part of a group.

Asking someone to hide or minimize any one of his/her identifiers is like asking someone to only celebrate certain aspects of his/her existence and ignore others. In other words, I can't be Black and not be a Black woman. I can't be a Black woman and not be over 40. I can't be a Black woman over 40 and not a small business owner. My race, gender, age, and employment status are linked and inseparable. This is who I am. I am always at the intersection of my identities.

And so are you. This, I have found, is what gives you an advantage. As you begin to execute your idea, remember that you are part of a group that had the courage and the faith to pivot. There are many reasons to stand proudly and you should.

Your Uniqueness is a Selling Point

I am not much of a movie person, but occasionally I will take a deep dive and acquaint myself with what's trending and what's current in the world of popular culture. And this has brought me to this year's Academy Award nominations. If last year was #oscarssowhite then this year seems to be #oscarssocolorful.

For the first time, there are actors/actresses of color nominated in every major category. A Black screenwriter and editor were also nominated. Typically, there are very few people of color recognized for their work at this level. Social media platforms like Twitter have erupted with glee that this year's nominations actually look more like America compared to the homogenous groups of years past. But, should we really be rejoicing?

I ask this question because it still concerns me that we are celebrating that which should come naturally to us—that which we should expect—that which should happen if we allowed the genius of creativity and art to guide our perceptions of greatness and not racial biases.

Unfortunately, this is also a concern in the world of freelancing. A while ago, an online discussion emerged as to whether or not Black business owners/freelancers should use images of people of color when advertising and marketing their services. Some argued that stock images of White people would be more universally appealing and would attract "mainstream" clients. They also felt that too many colorful images would alienate or deter potential White clients. Others contended that entrepreneurs of color should not have to hide behind stock images and they should not be burdened with solving a systemic problem that shouldn't even exist in 2019.

Sitting on a virtual bench watching people volley back and forth, I was a spectator in a conversation that was both enlightening and painful. I have never hidden the fact that I am a Black woman. My face is the profile picture on my business' Facebook page and I often write about the intersections of race, gender, culture, and identity.

As such, there were aspects of the conversation that simply did not resonate with me. I firmly believe that no one should erase or downplay his/her racial or ethnic background and the value of one's work should not be underestimated because of others' misconceptions about race or their implicit or expressed biases.

But I am also more seasoned than a 22-year-old who is just starting out and who wants to attract a diverse clientele. Hindsight being 20/20, I should have said this:

We still live in a society where some people will not give you a chance because of their prejudices associated with the color of your skin, especially in our current political climate.

I would never tell anyone to hide who you are, but be realistic. You will be googled and upon glancing at your picture—before clicking on a link—someone will decide to take their business elsewhere. Remember, this is not a reflection of your value or your worth.

Be confident in your craft. We don't often talk about what acts of racism and prejudice do to one's spirit. In the midst of dealing with it, you can't succumb to the idea that you, or your work, are less than. We ALL miss out when we diminish our own greatness to make others feel comfortable.

At times, you may not meet other entrepreneurs who look like you, but be encouraged that there are those who will act as allies, who will support you, and who will stand in solidarity for racial equity. Sincere advice, genuine respect, and authentic friendships can bridge differences.

I never believed in the idea of a post-racial society, but I do believe that we can become more of an equitable society. I often encourage members of underrepresented groups to become freelancers or creative entrepreneurs. Because of this, I would love to see more entrepreneurs who are truly free to just be themselves.

Be Uncompromising In Doing Things the Right Way for the Right Reasons

The bottom line is a concept that many of us have become accustomed to throughout our entrepreneurial journeys. In some instances, it determines the decisions that we make ranging from talent acquisition, operating expenses, and even merchandising budgets.

The bottom line
It is often a critical factor in determining whether a business is successful or not. So much so, that sometimes we, myself included, forget that the bottom line is not the only line that we should be concerned with, especially if we ignore other lines that have far greater societal implications and consequences.

And that leads me to a larger conversation about two lynchpin moments this week. Two of the largest and most popular corporations in America: Starbucks and ABC (whose parent company is Disney) drew a symbolic line about race relations in America.

The Starbucks effect
After a racially motivated incident at one of its stores in Philadelphia where a barista called the police on two Black male guests, Starbucks decided to close 8,000 of its stores for two hours on May 29th to implement an anti-bias training program for over 175,000 of its employers. It is estimated that doing so will cost Starbucks close to $14 million dollars in revenue.

On the same day that Starbucks closed for its training program, ABC announced that it was canceling the reboot of the Roseanne Show after its star and namesake, Roseanne, tweeted a vitriolic and racist tweet about Valerie Jarrett that included language, amongst other things, that compared her to an ape. With an estimated 40 million dollars in ad revenue being forfeited by axing the sitcom, a tsunami of conversations and debates erupted on cable TV, network news programs, and entertainment shows.

Many pundits and guests were utterly dismayed that ABC would cancel one of its biggest money earners. I can't tell you how often I heard people discuss or allude to the bottom line and the money that ABC would miss out on for first run advertisements and syndication deals.

In both of these instances, ABC and Starbucks could have issued a flowery apology and distanced themselves from their employees' words and actions. Instead, they opted to do something far more powerful—they used these very public moments of disgrace to show the rest of us that we cannot allow the bottom line to usurp our moral compass, not as individuals and not as institutions.

Doing the right thing is always worth the risk
When faced with the decision of doing the right thing, even when it is inconvenient and at great financial risk, we must do the right thing. This is not about politics or political correctness; this is about understanding the divisive times that we are in—a time that is governed by name calling, finger pointing, and defeatist talk. A time that in my 45 years on this planet has never been so polarized. [I am convinced that 30 years from now, historians will look back on this period and draw a clear line of demarcation about what it meant to be on the right side of history.]

Setting an example
Whether we are side hustlers, solopreneurs, or small business owners, what Starbucks and Disney did should serve as examples for all of us. What good is a moral compass if we are unwilling to use it? Many of us may not find ourselves dealing with catastrophes of this scale, but we may find ourselves having to decide whether or not a contract or project is worth potentially hurting or offending a demographic of people. Or we may find ourselves associated with people, business partners, or brands that are not aligned with our values.

Pivotal moments
The point is that we all have, or will have, pivotal moments in our lives where our decisions have tangible consequences and where our standing up for what is right has implications that are far more potent

than a sequence of zeroes on a balance sheet.

For these reasons, I applaud both Starbucks and ABC for making, what had to be, the difficult decision that no amount of revenue is worth the demoralization or dehumanizing of others. For those who say that their gestures were not enough, I simply say that a step in the right direction far outweighs no direction at all.

6

BRANDING YOURSELF: BY DESIGN OR BY DEFAULT?

Know Thyself

-Socrates (attribution)

Branding can either happen by design or by default. As entrepreneurs, it is important that we understand the power of our brand. It is even more important that we see ourselves as architects of that brand whether we are freelancers, contractors, sole proprietors or small business owners.

The cornerstone of most branding efforts is marketing. Traditionally, marketing was often connected to the print and visual ads that you might see in a newspaper, magazine, flyers, leaflets, brochures, TV commercials, billboards and/or radio ads. All of these methods still play a vital role in how information is disseminated and how brands are established and maintained. Yet, the advent of e-commerce and social media has drastically affected how we connect with each other and how we market to potential clients and customers.

For larger corporations, advertising and marketing are often significant line items in the budget. However, for smaller entities, including freelancers, there just may not be room in the budget. The good news is that size doesn't matter when it comes to effectively creating a brand and telling people about it.

Before you begin a marketing campaign, here are a few questions to consider: How much can I spend? What is my targeted audience? How can I reach this audience? Do I have the time, talent and resources to do the marketing myself or should I outsource it to another contractor?

Depending on the answers to these questions, you will be in a position to determine what your most immediate needs are and the best way to pursue those needs. In many instances, you may conclude that it is best to leave it to the experts. Others may find that branding and marketing can be handled in-house.

Because I opted for the latter, I'd like to share a few things with you that have worked for me and that have saved me money. In the spirit of full disclosure, everything that I learned about creating a brand and marketing was self-taught. It was also organic. I started by paying attention to the type of marketing content that caught my eye compared to the type that I discarded or ignored. I also focused on the aesthetics—how was the information presented. Lastly, I focused on what was said—the content. (Keep in mind that at some point, even if you launch on your own, you may still decide to outsource your marketing.)

After perusing the marketing materials of others, I discovered that traditional marketing would not be the best option for my line of work because 90% of my clients lived outside of my market. I needed to cast a much wider net and introduce my work to people in markets that extended far beyond my own.

This is where digital marketing entered my life. When you think digital marketing, think about the marketing that you have seen online on various websites and via platforms like Instagram, Facebook, Google, Twitter or even YouTube. Although the placement of some of these ads can be annoying, they do present advertisers with an opportunity to scale up their marketing efforts.

Of the digital options that I mentioned, the one that has led to the most leads and actual tangible sales has been via my company's Facebook page: Seldon Writing Group, LLC. I am intentional about using this page for the purposes of introducing and further branding the company. The posts are genuine and writing related. I often schedule months in advance to ensure that there is content on the page even if I am not online.

As a result of this digital marketing effort, Facebook clients now account for a significant number of our new clientele. I know others who have great results with Instagram Business and others who swear by LinkedIn. So, if Facebook is not your thing, you may want to think about another platform because, over time, the advantages add up and here's why:

Captive Audience: Even though potential clients can scroll over, hide, or ignore ads, there are also those who will read your content and follow-up. In this sense, you have a captive audience because digital marketing allows you to hone in on your desired audience. If you don't offer e-commerce, you can focus on your local demographic. If your products or services are geared towards a national and/or international audience then you can pitch to them. With Facebook, in particular, you can even specify an age range.

Engagement Options: With digital media, you can build rapport and relationships with your audience through your blogs, your posts, and your live videos. As you build up and maintain content, potential clients can decide which, if any, of these options they want to use to engage and stay connected with you. With smart devices—phones, tablets, and laptops, being ubiquitous in most communities, there is a strong possibility that someone will click. Once they click, it's up to you to convert that click into a sale.

Affordability: As I started to pay more attention to the "Sponsored" ads in my newsfeed, I assumed that they were expensive, but relatively speaking, they are not. Posts can be boosted (sponsored) for as little as $2 to $3 per day and you determine how long you want the ad to run.

Analytics: Data—some of us may be tired of hearing this word, but it is a critical aspect of any marketing campaign. No one wants to waste money or pour money into an effort that is futile. Empirically, data helps us measure whether or not we are generating the traffic that we desire and engaging with the clientele that we envisioned.

An added advantage is that I can compare the organic reach to the paid reach. This has helped me to determine which ads are worth boosting and how well a particular demographic responds to an ad. I then use that data for determining where to put my future digital marketing dollars. By tracking your reach and how many leads convert to sales, you can determine conversion rates; you can also determine if digital marketing is an optimal fit for you.

You are Your Brand

As I mentioned previously, I did not start this journey until I was in my late 30s. The beauty of this is that I made enough mistakes in my past careers that I did not enter into this world with unrealistic expectations or an overly romanticized vision of what this life might look like—besides being able to work from home in my PJs. I find that because I have launched a successful second career, people my age, and older, are intrigued by the idea of being a freelancer over the age of 40.

I tell people that the first time we do anything can be daunting. Even if we are well prepared, there is always the "what if" question that lingers. I recently had a virtual conversation with a witty older man who wants to be a freelance writer. He primarily uses his Facebook statuses as microblogs. With a strong following and positive feedback, he is ready to launch a public blog. His primary concern is that people outside of his immediate social circle might not "get him". My advice to him was to write in a way that is authentic and true. The most successful writers are ones who are honest or even vulnerable.

I told him that I struggle with people who use language not as a bridge to bring about greater understanding, but as a barrier. Unfortunately, there was a time in my life when that person was me. I wanted people to know that I was smart so I would intentionally use archaic words and revise my sentences to make them more complex and more convoluted. This was a carryover from my days as an academic. Yet, what worked in academia did not work in the blogosphere.

Lesson One: Transitioning to freelancing may require a new approach to your craft. Like many people who desire to speak or write for the public domain, I underestimated how much connecting with my audience mattered. I thought it was about me, my ideas, and my purpose. When this happens, and it happens too often, I think, we tend to see audience members as consumers and not potential converts. Yes, public writing is intended to be consumed—especially if a blog is monetized or a book is for sale—but, it is also supposed to be a conversation, albeit imaginary, between the writer and the reader.

Lesson Two: Not all projects will be right for a more mature freelancer. Whether it is a light-hearted topic or something more serious, there are times when a writer's age is a disadvantage; conversely, there are times when it is an advantage. Every once in a while, I am asked to contribute to an outlet whose target audience is millennials. Obviously, I am not a millennial—I have taught them; I mentor a few; and there are several in my family. My experience of writing for them is not the same as writing as one of them.

I made this clear to one editor and she told me that I probably wouldn't be a good fit because she needed someone with intimate knowledge about their everyday lives. I also did a pitch once for an outlet that wanted an article about the nuances of first-time homeownership. Albeit, it's been a while, but I was a first-time homebuyer 17 years ago. Needless to say, I didn't get any extra brownie points or that writing gig.

Lesson Three: You have a lot to share. Having the diverse life experiences that often come along with being older coupled with a willingness to speak openly about more complex topics is definitely an asset. So when I was pressed further by my 40+ year old FB friend about the advantages of freelancing, I told him to draw from his wealth of knowledge.

He asked me what should he do if "his truth" is difficult for others to accept. I responded that he should keep writing. Eventually he will find an audience that will embrace him and his writing style. The alternative—never writing for the public—is not an option. Of course, he, like others who are newer to freelancing, will grow along the way and he may even discover that he's not that hard to get after all. And that's the real beauty of being an older freelance writer. We can paint with a broad stroke or use the most intricate of brushes to tell stories, share experiences, and inform others.

What we can't do is pretend to be people who we are not which leads to the best advice that I can give to anyone launching a second career as a freelancer: Make sure that the voice that you use is your own. Eventually, everything else will fall into place.

Who Are You? Why Telling Your Story Matters

Stories have a way of drawing us in and making us feel connected, even with total strangers. There is something quite comforting about knowing that there is a natural human interest in learning more about people, especially the people we work with and in many instances, the people who contract with us to do work.

If you look through many of the lead stories in the news, magazine articles, or even top selling nonfiction books, there is a strong possibility that a compelling story is the nexus. For the same reason that readers and audience members gravitate towards these mediums, the power of your story can be a strong magnet for building your clientele. The keys are understanding why your story matters and why clients care.

Clients/customers are people too!

I was reminded of this recently when I was engaged in a phone consultation with a potential client. We'd never met and she was a referral from another client. After sharing with her my credentials, some of my work, and my philosophies about writing, she paused and asked, "Who are you?"

I knew exactly what she meant. She did not want an elevator pitch, a perfectly articulated biography or a laundry list of success stories—she wanted to know who I *really* was. So, I told her my story. I told her about Tyra and why I love helping people write and why the articulation and preservation of stories is critical, especially for underrepresented communities.

She was a corporate executive and after my bleeding-heart spill, I wondered if I told her too much information (TMI) or if it was so personal that it bordered on being unprofessional, but it was my truth and she did ask. As we wrapped up the conversation, she uttered the three words that many entrepreneurs love to hear, "I trust you." I thanked her and we proceeded to discuss the logistics and formalities of her project.

The trust factor
For those of you who conduct much of your work virtually or electronically compared to those who deal with clients in-person, your story is even more important to tell. The in-person and even brick and mortar entrepreneur may have a slight advantage because clients can pay attention to body language, affect, and even a person's energy. It is difficult to replicate this on the phone or even during virtual sessions.

So even if sharing your story does not come naturally to you, it is worth becoming more comfortable with peeling back a layer. Honestly, there was a time in my freelancing career when I would have hesitated to open up with a stranger. I would have stuck to my pseudo-scripted text. Time and wisdom have taught me that people value human connections and they appreciate realness. This, in turn, helps to build trust. So even though it took some time, I have learned to embrace the idea that when dealing with strangers, trust and respect are just as important as the quality of your product and your pricing.

So, what does telling your story look like?
There are several ways that we can tell our stories. If you use social

media platforms, you can provide snapshots of who you are as it relates to your expertise and services. This does not mean that you have to divulge overly personal information about your family and vacations, but you do want to share your story about your journey or why you started. This will help you avoid coming across as sterile or cookie cutter. Whether we accept it or not, potential clients are vetting us.

If social media is not in your wheelhouse, take advantage of telling your story in the "About Us" or "About Me" section of your website. I recommend that you maintain a formal tone, but still give potential clients a glimpse of who you are, why you care, and why they should secure your services.

If you use job boards to secure projects, then think of the most creative and concise way to stand out. When I taught, I had my creative writing students do an exercise where they had to write their memoirs in 6 words or less.

Relationships Matter
Telling your story may not come naturally for you and honestly, this may not seem important for all industries, but it is. The way you present your story can actually be a deal maker or a deal breaker for potential clients. This is not to suggest that you can always control how people perceive you, but it is to say that you can control your own narrative.

The most important variable is being honest. Every day, I see people who are emulating other people's styles and even their branding strategies. Although this may be effective short term, it is not the best approach if sustainability is on your radar. Transparency is important when interacting with potential clients who may become long-term clients because, as we all know, relationships matter.

Remember, it is not uncommon for potential clients to vet you. If you are consistent, relevant, reliable, and relatable then you have set the tone for future business interactions and transactional exchanges.

Tyra L. Seldon, Ph.D.

Protecting Your Work is Protecting Your Brand

Imagine that you've spent a considerable amount of time creating your version of a masterpiece. Whether it is a painting, a book, a musical score, software, or a graphic design logo, a freelancer's craft is often a reflection of their time, resources, and talents. There is also the monetary value that is attached to your work or intellectual property.

What is Intellectual Property?
Intellectual property is commonly and simply defined as a work or invention that is the result of one's mind or creativity. With the proliferation of social media and the ease of digitizing one's work, we often share or even overshare our intellectual property without thinking about the implications. Now, imagine the aforementioned masterpiece being stolen by someone else.

Innocuous Mistake or Something Else?
A few years ago, I posted a micro-blog on my personal page. It took me about an hour to write and it addressed a topic that I was deeply passionate about. My intent was simply to provide my take on an issue that was trending on Facebook. Because I wanted to respond in a timely manner, I decided to post it on FB rather than on my blog site. No big deal.

A couple of days later, a post came through my newsfeed. When I first read it, I thought, "Wow, what is the likelihood that this person would have the same exact sentiments about this particular subject matter?" I looked at his post more carefully. Not only were our ideas eerily similar but so was our diction, our syntax, and the overall way in which we expressed our ideas.

Then, I pulled my head out of the sand: Those were my words attributed to someone else on his page.

I went to the person's page and lo and behold, it became quite clear that he had copied and pasted what I said as if it were his own. I politely messaged him and attached a side-by-side screenshot of his post and mine. I asked him if he would attribute the content back to my page. If not, I asked that he take it down.

He apologized profusely and agreed to add the attribution. I was satisfied with how he handled it, but the experience left me with an unsettled feeling. If his post hadn't come through my newsfeed, I would not have known. I still believed that it was an innocuous mistake (although another part of me wanted to go into full English professor mode and have a serious discussion about plagiarism).

Yes, this was just a FB micro-blog, but it's the principle that matters. What about larger, more complex works or pieces that are not intended for dissemination on social media platforms? Property is property and no one likes to have their work used without permission or proper compensation. As a freelancer, what can you do to protect yourself?

What Type of Content Should be Copyrighted?
Content–such as fiction and non-fiction books, lyrics, jingles, periodicals, 2D and 3D artwork, drawings, apps, computer programs, animation, television shows, and commercial photos–is often copyrighted. Although this list isn't exhaustive, it is a good starting point. If you are a freelancer who creates in one of these areas, consider copyrighting your work.

Most creative content is copyrighted after it has been completed/produced. It is also worth noting that if you use a third party for the distribution or publishing of your work (e.g. a book self-publishing company) the company may take care of copyrighting your work on your behalf—just be sure to confirm this.

What are the Advantages of Copyrighting Your Work?
The advantage of copyrighting your work is that you are protecting yourself in case there are issues later on about rightful ownership and possible infringement. It alleviates doubt as to who owns the work and when the work was originally created. The Library of Congress explains:

"Registration is recommended for a number of reasons. Many choose to register their works because they wish to have the facts of their copyright on the public record and have a certificate of registration. Registered works may be eligible for statutory damages and attorney's fees in successful litigation. Finally, if registration occurs within five years of publication, it is considered prima facie evidence in a court of law. See Circular 1, Copyright Basics, section "Copyright Registration" and Circular 38b, Highlights of Copyright Amendments Contained in the Uruguay Round Agreements Act (URAA), on non-U.S. works."

Creative entrepreneurs in particular must be careful. Being diligent about protecting your intellectual and creative property may require a few extra steps, but being proactive is worth avoiding the heartache of potentially being tied up in litigation years later.

How Can You Protect Your Work?
Protecting your work can actually be a DIY endeavor. Depending on the nature of your content, you may want to consider registering your work with the Library of Congress. The fees are nominal depending on what you are copyrighting. Although ownership begins with creation, it is important, in my opinion, to have a paper trail.

Contrary to popular belief, the poor man's copyright, or emailing/mailing content to yourself to get a date and time stamp, is not recommended. The Library of Congress notes that, "There is no provision in the copyright law regarding any such type of protection, and it is not a substitute for registration."

If copyrighting is not the best option for your work, you may want to think about trademarking or patenting it. The United States Patent and Trademark Office provides extensive information as to what content should be trademarked or patented and the process for doing so.

And if you are not sure if you need one, or all three, check out: https://www.uspto.gov/. This is a valuable resource that differentiates between trademarks, patents, and copyright.

Lastly, there is always the option of seeking a good intellectual property lawyer. Whatever you decide to do, remember it's your property and you want to protect it. Operating under the assumption of good will may not be enough, especially with downloading, sharing, and reposting being so ubiquitous in our society.

7

BUSINESS OR EXPENSIVE HOBBY?

A person always doing his or her best becomes a natural leader by example.

-Joe DiMaggio

When I entered the entrepreneurial ecosystem, I did so with great intentionality. I wanted to monetize my writing skills. As I have mentioned in previous chapters, I now mentor quite a few younger writers who want to become professional writers. The first thing that I tell them is that this is a business. Yes, you have a gift and yes, you are passionate and yes, the world needs to hear your story, but you also need to be clear about your services. Your creativity, your intellect, your skills, and your personality are all valuable assets.

Although monetization is not the only goal, you do need to be mindful of whether or not you really want to execute and sustain a business or if it is an expensive hobby.

It is so tempting in this age of e-commerce and my "friend's friend" to simply take a job post or a request from a stranger at face value. But this is dangerous and can lead to exploitation, especially for people who are learning how to navigate the vast sea that we call entrepreneurship.

As I help my mentees to take their first swim, I am starting to notice the frequency in which horror stories are emerging about business owners who either aren't getting paid or their payments are long overdue. Hence the title, "Freelancing Ain't Free Nor Should It Be."

One recent story was particularly disturbing. If you are Black (or are familiar with Black culture) and you have lived in America from the 1960s through the early 2000s, then there is a strong possibility that a copy of *Ebony*, and her sister publication *Jet*, was somewhere on a coffee table, a night stand, or in a magazine rack in your home, your neighbor's home, and all of the Black enterprises that you frequented that had waiting rooms. Yes, *Ebony* was that ubiquitous in Black communities. In fact, it was the pride and glory of all Black publications. If your picture and/or your story made it into this esteemed magazine then you had arrived.

So, when I discovered that one of the most iconic Black magazine outlets was allegedly not paying some of its writers, my mouth, literally, dropped. In 2017 an article by a young writer of color, Jagger Blaec, spells out that there were, reportedly, several Black writers who had not been paid for their published work, some dating as far back as 2013. As of the writing of this book in 2019, some people still have not received compensation for their work.

In the spirit of transparency, this is hard to believe not because I don't believe Jagger Blaec and the writers who started the movement, but because I have always held *Ebony* to a higher standard. It is not a start-up. It has a long-standing brand. At one point, it was a multi-million-dollar entity. More importantly, if anyone should do right by its Black writers, it's a medium that would not even exist without its Black readership.

My point in bringing this up is not to single out just *Ebony* because I know that this has happened with other print and digital publications. With this particular story, the author notes that many of the Black writers have been eerily quiet or have just waited for everything to work itself out. Of course, most of us do not desire to take legal action, but no freelancer should ever accept being exploited by anyone. Period.

This is why it is so important for new start-ups and freelancers to advocate for themselves and to have the terms of their contracts honored, even if it means taking legal action. New York City was the first to pass the historic Freelance Isn't Free Act, which went into effect on May 15, 2018.

Under this new legislation, clients will have to use contracts when working with a freelancer, and they will now face double damages, attorney's fees, and other penalties for nonpayment. Stories like these illustrate just why we need this law, and why we should be working together to get it passed across the nation.

Unpaid invoices are the underbellies of entrepreneurship. Not talking about it will not make it go away. Just as many of us had zero tolerance for inequity in corporate spaces, we must bring that same tenacity to the world of freelancing.

Fully executing an idea can be extremely hard work. It is rare that the work comes to you; often, you have to go find it. Part of the difficulty is knowing where to look for legitimate projects. There are numerous sites that proclaim to help people launch their businesses, but "buyer beware" because not all sites are clear about how they connect writers to projects or the nature of those projects.

Having been in business for almost 8 years, I am cautious of any site that requires me to "pay" to have access to common information. However, I fell for this when I first started and I don't want you to make the same mistake.

Be leery of business coaching/consulting that is ambiguous in scope or that promises large payouts, but gives very little information on the front end. There is, unfortunately, a fertile market for scammers and people who may take advantage of your eagerness and desire to start a business.

Because of my background in academia, I won't even entertain anything that remotely smells of dishonesty or fraud. Because of this, I recommend that you read the fine print and ask questions before signing up. If it doesn't feel right, trust your gut.

If you are clear about what to avoid, it makes it easier to focus on what you really want and that is a successful launch. Here are a few things that I highly recommend during the execution stage:

Sign up for newsletters and email blasts from reputable organizations. One of my favorites is Freedom With Writing. I find that they have thoroughly vetted writing opportunities before sharing them with their large following. They also highlight outlets that are not mainstream or popularly known; this is particularly helpful for writers who tend to write about niche topics or for targeted audiences.

Additionally, they tend to share writing gigs that pay significantly more than some other writing sites. I have acquired a few contracts through their information. Did I mention that they will email writing opportunities directly to you?

Don't underestimate traditional job search engines. This may be surprising, but with the right key words, you can actually get a few paid writing gigs using sites like Monster, CareerBuilder, and Indeed. Of these three, Indeed is my favorite. On a few occasions, I have used words like "writer," "editor," "curriculum," "script," and/or a major city like New York, LA, Chicago.

Even though I don't live in these cities, I have found that short-term or one-time writing projects or contracts are more bountiful in larger markets. I have also used "remote" as my location. As with anything else, do your research to make sure that the projects are legitimate. Also, be sure that you are clear about how payments will be made—if it sounds too good to be true, then follow your instinct.

Guest blog and create content for other platforms, especially national ones. Please don't stop reading! Hear me out. When you first start writing, many of the larger outlets that accept unsolicited pitches will want to know who you are and others will ask for published samples or a writing portfolio. Your favorite blog in a Word document will not suffice as a writing sample.

Private and corporate clients also want to know that you have experience writing for an audience, so it's not just a function of showing them that you are a good writer, but they also want to see how you engage with an audience. Because of this, I strongly recommend writing for an occasional byline (where your name is included, tagged and/or you are able to include a short biography) if an outlet does not pay its writers.

The other important thing about writing for a byline is that you can leverage an outlets' reach (readers and followers) and brand to gain greater visibility as you establish your identity as a professional writer. You, literally, never know who will read your content and the doors that might open for you.

Join online groups. I joined a FB group after someone read one of my blogs on *Freelancer's Union* and she emailed me about it. It has turned out to be a gold mine, as I am able to listen and learn from people who have far more experience than I do. I also have a writing group comprised of aspiring and established writers.

I use the metaphor of a table to describe it—sometimes you come to the table because you are hungry and you desire to eat and on other occasions, you come because you want to feed others. Writing groups, entrepreneurs' groups/unions, and/or "support" groups for writers are great ways to make connections, give/receive referrals, and learn about job leads that are not posted in more public spaces.

How Projecting Can Save You From Trouble Later

One of the ways that you can effectively execute your business is sitting down (or standing up) and mapping out your budget. If you prefer to chunk the year out in quarters instead of plotting the entire year, go for it! Regardless of the methodology, be sure to plan ahead. Planning ahead involves projecting, or anticipating, your expenses and your revenue. It also involves guess work, analytics, and maybe, some optimism, yet it is doable and I highly recommend forecasting your budget, especially for new entrepreneurs. Here's how:

Focus on What You Do Know: The first time I projected a budget, I was overly optimistic, to the point of being unrealistic. I included revenue that was based upon wishful thinking and not facts. Instead of honing in on what I did know about my job patterns, I focused on what I wanted them to be. The prior year, I had 12 clients and I was projecting that I would uptick to 200 clients for the next fiscal year.

Was this possible? Sure, but it was highly improbable. The budget I forecasted was futile which defeated the purpose of creating a budget in the first place. Thankfully, I had a mentor who reviewed it and simply asked: "Where are *all* of these extra clients coming from?" I did not have a satisfactory answer.

I wanted the extra clients, but I did not have a plan. So, I revamped my budget and focused on the variables that I could most accurately predict. I made it more realistic based upon my market, my previous year's earnings, my marketing strategy, and the number of leads and potential clients that I had in the pipeline.

And it worked! The forecasted budget was just slightly off from my actual budget for that year. The takeaway: Your prior knowledge and experience are invaluable tools for creating a budget.

Take Advantage of Tools: The good news is that you don't have to figure everything out by yourself. There are numerous resources, tools, and apps that can serve as templates to help you manage your finances and plan your budget for the year. One list that I found to be helpful includes tools that not only help with budgeting, but also with planning for taxes, and methods for sending and receiving money: https://www.upwork.com/hiring/community/8-helpful-finance-apps-for-freelancers-small-business-owners/.

Not everything in this list will be necessary for planning your yearly budget, but you may find that there are resources here that may be beneficial in the future. Think about bookmarking it, just in case.

Trust the Professionals: As much as I want you to save money, I must also tell you that DIY and apps are not for everyone. Honestly, numbers are not my thing; I even regret not paying more attention during my high school and collegiate math courses. Thankfully, there are trained professionals who are well-versed and experienced with working with budgets, especially the more complicated ones. As your business expands, I highly recommend that you seek out a CPA or a bookkeeper who can literally either walk you through the process or even do it for you.

The advantage of using a hired professional is that he/she will have a deeper understanding of state and federal tax laws, how to earmark expenses, how to plan your payroll, how to identify tax deductions, and what constitutes charitable giving—all of which can factor into your 2019 budget. Additionally, if you are able to contract with a freelance CPA, there is a greater likelihood that he/she will truly understand what you do and some of the nuances that go into a freelancer's budget.

Saving Money: How does all of this lead to saving money? By focusing on what you do know, you will be able to create a budget that actually works. Every year thereafter, use a strategy that helps you stay within your allocated budget and not overspend.

Impulsive spending, purchasing unnecessary supplies, and even over-hiring are often antithetical to profitability and growth. In this sense, projecting your budget can help you save money now and in years to come. It can also help you anticipate reasonable growth.

More than anything, creating a budget forces you to be realistic about what you can spend, when you can spend it and how you spend it. The more that you are able to project and operate within your specified parameters, the more likely you are to save. In other words, the more you budget, the more you eventually profit.

Are you Ready to Convert a Lead Into a Sale?

The coveted sale often serves as an end goal for many of us. But, in the process of focusing on a sale, we may be neglecting the importance of a lead and more importantly, how to convert a lead into an actual sale. Although every potential client will not become a client, there are some strategies that entrepreneurs can use to better position themselves to be successful.

1. Recognize a Lead When You See One—Traditionally, we may think of a lead as being an overt or explicit expression of interest in our services, including a referral from a client. This type of lead is still viable, but there are some leads that are not as obvious.

A subtle comment by an acquaintance, an ISO (in search of) on social media, or a passing conversation amongst friends/colleagues can be opportunities to explain what you do and to promote your work. These are the types of leads that are easy to miss or ignore. However, think of them as implicit leads or as untapped opportunities. Because someone has not explicitly expressed interest in your services, it doesn't mean that there isn't still an opportunity to follow-up in an appropriate manner.

For example, a stranger on FB posted that he was finishing up the last chapter of a book. I sent him a congratulatory inbox message. I also told him about our editing services and sent him a link to our website. I asked him to consider us for his future copy-editing needs. The message was sincere and concise.

I saw planting this seed as creating a bridge. I also saw it as a lead even though that probably was not the intent of his post. By sending the inbox, I was establishing a relationship (see number 2 below). I knew that the worst-case scenario was a "no." Instead, he did check out the website and he, eventually, became a client.

The key is not to be overly aggressive or pushy, but to sincerely establish an opportunity to stay connected. Some people will be receptive and others will not. Focus on the people who are receptive. On numerous occasions, including the aforementioned one, I have seen leads generated from casual connections (coupled with appropriate follow-up) convert to sales.

2. Build and Nurture the Relationship—No matter how great you are or how great your service/products are, that pales in comparison to the importance of establishing healthy relationships with potential clients. When responding to a lead, something as simple as: "How are you?" or "I hope all is well" can set the tone for future interactions.

The best way to think about this is to think about your role as a consumer. When you are seeking out a vendor, business, or even fellow freelancer, what makes you contract/support one person over another?

It is not always about the product. Often our decisions start and end with our relationship with the person with whom we are doing business: Do I feel valued? Am I treated with respect? Do I trust this person? When the answers to these questions are in the affirmative, we are able to make connections, business or otherwise.

Because most leads may not know us personally or they may only be peripherally familiar with our work, the initial interaction is an opportunity to build a relationship. What we do beyond that will foster the relationship. This is of particular importance for multiple-step projects, long-term projects, and multiple project contracts. In other words, that one 'yes' can be a launching pad for several more.

3. Respond in a Timely Manner—At one point, I relied too heavily on my company's FB page. Potential clients would inbox me and I would respond 2 to 3 days later. In at least one instance, someone was gracious enough to tell me that my lack of timeliness in responding led to her seeking someone else. I didn't think 2 to 3 days was a long span of time, but from her vantage point, it was. I speculate that she thought that my lack of timeliness and urgency was a reflection of how I would have handled her project—lesson learned.

Ostensibly, social media has conditioned some potential clients to expect to have 24/7 access, so some people desire immediacy in how we respond to their requests (e.g. for a quote, for a consultation, for answers to clarifying questions). Sometimes, those expectations are unrealistic. Therefore, I recommend that if you have a website that you redirect people to it and that you implement a 24 hour reply rule which simply means that someone will respond to all web-based inquiries within 24 hours.

If you don't have a website, include verbiage about your response process on your business social media pages, your email automatic response, or on your flyers and blog posts: "All inquiries will be addressed…" Some entrepreneurs even opt for personal assistants or virtual assistants to help them manage potential leads.

The key is that you recognize the importance of someone else's time and the value of an inquiry. He/she took the time to reach out to you for a reason. When a potential client feels as if they are important and that you value his/her time, there is a greater likelihood that, all things considered, you will close the deal. Remember, your follow-up is a reflection of your follow-through.

Lessons Learned
To be honest, when I first started, I was not very good at converting leads to sales. In fact, even today, sales/marketing are the most difficult aspects of freelancing and business ownership. My company is still too small to justify outsourcing it, so in many ways, I learned about sales because I had to.

Initially, I erroneously thought that if people were interested, they would hire me. This was a relatively passive approach that led to few conversions and much frustration. As my life as a freelancer has evolved, so too has my attitude about sales. Now, I better understand that people are often shopping around. They are seeking the best fit, the right person, or the right product.

Even if you are not gifted in sales, who knows what you do better than you do? So, the next time you get a lead, implicit or explicit, remember that you can effectively close the deal.

Thinking about the Bigger Picture

As a customer, I love the old adage, "The customer is always right." As a freelancer, I am not as enamored with it. In fact, I find that if one is not careful, this can create contentious relationships and lead to unrealistic expectations.

When I first started, a woman reached out to me to inquire about my ghostwriting services. She was a first-time author who wanted to capture her life story in a memoir. We had a delightful phone conversation and I was ready to close the deal. As we began to wrap up, she said, "Now, can you guarantee me that my book will be a New York Time's Best Seller?"

My words came out of my mouth before I could censor them, "Absolutely not and if someone makes you that promise, you need to run. Run like Forrest Gump!"

I never heard from her again and to be honest, it was probably for the best. Can you imagine the roller coaster ride that we would have embarked upon if she went into the writing process with that demand? Now, I am not advocating that you walk away from business, but I am a strong proponent of maintaining your emotional, spiritual, creative, and intellectual well-being.

And let's be brutally honest, some clients can be difficult, especially if they have unrealistic expectations about your work. And as my late father used to say, "All money is not good money."

And that can lead to a conundrum for those of us who freelance. How do you determine if a project is going to be worth it? Do you walk away from a great opportunity simply because it may require a little extra energy, more diplomacy, or even greater patience and charm?

I have found that the key is communicating with my clients at the very beginning before contracts have been signed and tasks have been performed. Before taking any writing or editing job, I ask my clients to clearly express their goals for the project at hand. Sometimes these goals are straightforward and easily conveyable; in other instances, even the client isn't sure what she is asking of me. In those cases, we brainstorm together and I capture everything in writing. The same language is then ported over into the contract.

Although this process takes time, it provides the freelancer with a chance to make sure that the expectations are clear and everyone is on the same page. It also allows you to determine if a project is feasible or if you have the capacity to do it.

But let me forewarn you that even with all of the precautions in the world, you will still encounter clients who may make unrealistic demands or complain about the quality or caliber of your work.

I had another first-time author who was quite young and excitable. I explained to him the editing process that I use. Everything was spelled out and documented. Each step of the way, he was looped in and asked to sign off on the changes that I made. However, when it was time to sign off on the final proof of his book galley, he generated a list of things that he wanted me to tweak.

My first inclination was to send him a long trail of emails with highlights of my confirming that he was satisfied with the progression of the project. Then I thought about sending him the contract. Legally, I had fulfilled our contractual obligation as spelled out in the terms that he agreed upon and signed off on.

Making the changes that he was asking for would require additional time. When I indicated that there would be an additional fee, he confessed that he had not read all of my correspondences carefully. He apologized profusely. This was his first book. He was new to all of this.

I thought deeply about what I should do next. Even when running a business, there has to be some room for grace. Billy Joel once sang, "You're only human. You're allowed to make your share of mistakes."

We are only human and so are our clients. There are occasions, like with this young man, where we have to decide if being right is worth it. In this case, I simply made the corrections he asked for and I didn't charge him. He was happy. But, he wasn't right.

Ramping Up Your Business

I love the springtime. There is something about watching nature shift from being dormant to being in full bloom that warms my heart. It also serves as a reminder that it's time to start cleaning, but not just my yard and my home. Yes, proverbial spring cleaning can also apply to your business.

As you are ramping up and growing, I recommend that you reflect, plan, purge, and forge ahead. As you evaluate your wheelhouse, you may discover that you want to change a few things or you may want to ramp up your business. Think about your marketing plan, take some online classes and/or attend a few workshops. Also follow up with potential clients who may have previously inquired about your services.

Just as the ramping up season is an opportunity for you to plant metaphorical flowers, it is equally as important that you don't create a breeding ground for weeds. In other words, you don't want to do something this spring that will have a negative ripple effect throughout the rest of the year.

Here are three things to avoid this spring and throughout the rest of your planning and planting season:

Speaking negatively about the competition: This may seem odd as the first item on this list, but I am seeing quite a bit of this, so I wanted to get it out of the way. This is the kind of weed that can kill even the strongest strains of grass. Putting someone else's work down does not automatically mean that someone will see your work as being better. Instead, it can come across as unprofessional, brash, and even toxic. Most clients want great service, not drama.

Even in an attempt to be helpful by pointing out someone else's flaws, making disparaging comments about your competition, especially fellow entrepreneurs, reflects poorly on you. Instead of highlighting or identifying what someone else is not good at, focus, instead, on what you can do and how your services are a good fit for a client.

Outpricing the market: "You charge too much." "You don't charge enough." This may feel like a game of tug-of-war without a winner. It is highly probable that you have quoted two different clients the same price for the same service and their reactions were diametrically opposed. What's a freelancer to do?

When our prices are too high, someone may think that we are overpriced in order to create an outrageous profit margin. Conversely, if our prices are too low, a client may think that we are inexperienced or amateurs. The solution? Become familiar with your industry's pricing standards.

There are unions and professional organizations that will often openly share information about median wages or price points for services that are similar to the ones that you offer. Before you spike up your prices this spring, become familiar with wage guides and use them as starting points; obviously, allow some flexibility as geography often is a determining factor in what people are willing to pay for certain services.

If you charge $100.00 an hour, but the going rate in your area for the same service is $50.00, just understand that you may be outpricing your services. No matter how good you are, you have to understand your market.

Overselling and underperforming: I saved the best for last. If we are honest, freelancing can be highly competitive, especially in certain markets. As such, many of us are looking for something that makes us stand out or that gives us a slight advantage over our peers.

Perhaps you have thought about offering a client an ancillary service for free, or you plan to guarantee that a product will be ready for a client in four days when it normally takes seven. Maybe you plan to create a price-matching program where you will honor or beat a quoted rate. These things all look great on paper.

But, here's the problem: Can you deliver? Do you have the capacity, resources, stamina, time, and availability to make good on the deliverables that you have promised? If the answer is no, then it's best that you don't overcommit or oversell.

Trust is one of the most important components of building a business. Your clients depend upon you and trust you. Once a client no longer trusts you, it is incredibly difficult, if at all possible, to rebuild that trust.

Instead, allow the natural progression or process to unfold and be transparent with your clients. That extra three days you were going to knock off are probably not that big of a deal, especially if the quality of work is compromised.

Mistakes to Avoid Throughout the Execution Phase

I am a researcher, so when I started freelancing in my late thirties, one of the first things that I did was research freelancing. Almost everything I read was geared towards much younger entrepreneurs or those who were launching their first careers. There were numerous pieces about getting experience, building a brand, and leveraging social media to build one's clientele.

All of this was valuable and proved to be helpful at various stages during my transition, but I wasn't receiving what I needed.

I didn't want to freelance just to freelance. I didn't want to freelance because it was a fun hobby. I didn't want to freelance just to survive. I wanted to freelance to thrive and to sustain the quality of life that I had grown accustomed to as an academic. I'm allergic to the starving artist mantra.

Then reality hit. There were many opportunities, but the pay was very low.

One night, I even calculated how many low paying articles I would have to write in a week just to make a fraction of what I was making before. My heart sunk—maybe I was being foolish and this life was not for me, at least not at my age. Clearly, I was doing something wrong. I had the skill set; I had a portfolio full of diverse samples;

and I had a vision, but the income was not coming in. Something was missing.

I assumed that with my credentials and years of experience, I simply had to let people know that I was now freelancing and they would respond accordingly. Wrong!

I am not an essentialist, so I don't believe that only people of a certain group can speak about/for that group. However, real-world life experiences sprinkled with candor carry far more weight than an intriguing internet article. So I reached out to a dear friend who had also left academia and launched a successful second career as a creative independent in his early 40s.

As I explained my level of frustration and expressed a desire to just quit, he listened attentively. As the conversation unfolded, I realized that I was making several mistakes.

I was being too restrictive and I needed to diversify the types of writing projects and clients that I wanted to work with. The nature of freelancing is such that, for many of us, we can live anywhere and work from anywhere. I was concentrating too much on building up my local clientele. Yes, I am in the Midwest; however, I have a service that is of value for people on the coasts, places in-between, and overseas. I had to rethink how I was marketing my services and to whom I was marketing them to.

I was only focusing on two types of freelancing—academic and curriculum writing. It dawned on me that I had also developed pretty acute editing skills (all of those years of grading English papers and teaching grammar in intro to writing courses), so I added editing to my toolbox of services. This created an additional stream of income. I cannot emphasize enough the importance of having diverse income streams—some people even refer to these as profit centers. The value of this is that if one area is not producing enough income, you will still have revenue coming in from another stream of income. And this brings me to the biggest mistake that many of us make during this stage of our journey.

Entrepreneurship is not the same as working for someone else. When you have worked within a system for most of your adult life, you grow accustomed to the processes that work within that system. For example, having a supervisor, having structure, having a built-in accounting system, earning paid time off, receiving merit pay, and enjoying cost of living increases are often outgrowths of working for someone else in America.

When you strip away that system and find yourself in a new space, you have to change your way of thinking. I had to think about writing as art and as commerce. If I wanted to enjoy the benefits of writing as a business, I had to treat it as a business enterprise. This meant that I had to create systems. Why? If you build it, they still may not come but when they do, you need to be ready.

All of these mistakes were preventable, but I really didn't know that at the time. They were valuable, yet costly, exercises that reinforced that what worked in the academic/education space (my first career) would not necessarily work in the world of free enterprise.

So, before you launch your second career as a freelancer, take the time to find someone who has a track record of doing what you desire to do. Seek the advice or counsel of other entrepreneurs. Learn from that person's mistakes and successes. I know one conversation, when I was on the cusp of giving up, was the turning point for me.

Purpose and Passion Can be Mutually Inclusive

"I want to make a lot of money," my friend said as we wrapped up a conversation about her life goals.

She continued with a quizzical look on her face, "There's nothing wrong with that, right?"

I replied, "Of course, not. There is nothing wrong with wanting to make money."

Truth be told, I did cringe a bit when she said it, not because I was being dishonest, but because it is rare to hear someone say it. We tend to condition ourselves to think that our life's work should align to higher causes or noble ideas like helping people or solving problems. We often tie our aspirational goals to impact and purpose.

However, there is an elephant in the room and it's called money. And we need to start talking about it.

It doesn't help that money has gotten a pretty bad wrap in popular culture and society in general. Songs like "For the Love of Money," "Mo'Money, Mo'Problems," "Money," "Money for Nothing," "Eat the Rich" and "Money, Money, Money" reflect decades of music, a mosaic of artists, and diverse genres; yet, each one gives us a glimpse into our mercurial relationship with money. Compound this with the proverbial saying that money is the root of all evil and it becomes more evident as to why we shy away from having honest conversations about it.

It is so ingrained in us to not talk about money that the silence has become normative. If you ever worked in a corporate or institutional setting, you probably remember the unwritten rule about not talking about salaries. Many of us walked around with blinders on and assumed that our peers were making the same amount of money as we were for the same amount of work.

Furthermore, if you dare ask most Americans about their socio-economic class, they will probably tell you that they are middle class. If you dig further, the middle-class moniker is so ubiquitous that thousands of dollars and hundreds of zip codes separate us. (I'll never forget the time that I was teaching a course and a student whose parents made $80,000 sat beside one whose parents made over $2 million and they both identified as middle class.) There is some comfort in all of us being middle class. Why? Because once again, we don't have to talk about money.

And here's why that is problematic for freelancers and entrepreneurs. When we don't talk about money, we minimize its importance in our lives. When we don't talk about money, we inadvertently contribute to systems that allow money to create barriers and divisions, especially as it relates to salaries and compensation for women and people of color. When we don't talk about money, we tend to devalue the worth of our goods, products, and/or services. When we don't talk about money, we sometimes allow others to disempower us.

Just writing that last paragraph was demoralizing. But it doesn't have to be that way. Because we, entrepreneurs, often enjoy certain levels of autonomy and independence, we are actually perfectly positioned to have these conversations, especially with one another. When I first started, I was clueless about how much to charge. I carried over that corporate (academia for me) mindset about not talking about money. I just figured that I would Google a few things and go from there. Google is great, but it it's not a substitution for a real, human being.

Now, I will pick up the phone, shoot an email, or inbox someone to gain greater clarity about how much a project is worth, if I should present a counter offer, and/or if the compensation is fair. And, I have even gotten bold enough to ask, "How much did you charge for that service?" I have been amazed and thankful at the frequency in which people have shared this information. In turn, I have shared it with other entrepreneurs. What this does is demystify aspects of the f entrepreneurship process. It also empowers producers, which all of us as entrepreneurs are, to have honest dialogues about money.

We need money. We want it and we've put in the work to earn it. So, at the very least, let's talk about it.

Entrepreneurship: A Trend or a Calling

If you are a hip-hop aficionado or someone who is remotely familiar with popular culture then you've probably heard the buzz surrounding Jay-Z's t album, *4:44*.

My musical tastes are quite eclectic, so I don't profess to be an expert, but I will say that there were elements of Jay-Z's entire album that really resonated with me as an entrepreneur, especially his discussions surrounding credit, ownership, and generational wealth. Listening to his album really made me think about the importance of messaging about entrepreneurship.

If you peruse most major financial publications like Forbes and WSJ, there is quite a bit of hype surrounding entrepreneurship. These outlets tend to be geared towards individuals who are formally educated, highly trained, and experienced in their industries.

Juxtapose that with *4:44* and it's self-evident that its audience is slightly more nuanced and diverse—this is not to say that WSJ subscribers don't also love hip hop. My point is that different mediums and messengers use different tools to reach their targeted audiences. Regardless of one's age and education level, many of us see entrepreneurship as a chance to claim our slice of the American pie and live the quintessential American Dream.

As much as I love this push to increase entrepreneurship and make people more aware, I also think that it's important to not make it seem as if it's so easy, because it's not. In fact, being an entrepreneur is the most difficult thing that I have ever done. Six years in the game—as they say—and I am still figuring out how to navigate this space.

My point is that the pathway to entrepreneurship does not come with a universal GPS that leads everyone down the same road. In fact, sometimes the GPS may warn: Unknown roads ahead, proceed with caution (I actually encountered this for the first time over the weekend while driving in squares—not circles, but squares—in a small southern town).

Similar to my driving experience, there are many of us who enter this space not sure of where we are going; we just know that we are heading somewhere and that we will eventually get there, even if it's not the way we planned. Along the journey, some of us decide that entrepreneurship is not for us. Some do it because a traditional work space is not an option, and others, like myself, are so deeply passionate about what we do that we figure the business "stuff" out along the way.

Between *4:44* and my second quarter (which was horrible with contracts falling through, unpaid invoices, and promises unkept), I have been thinking a lot about what it really takes to stick to this.

More than anything, entrepreneurship requires commitment. No matter how skilled you are or how innovative your services or products are, you must have the fortitude to stick with your game plan or revise it if it no longer works for you.

Like many of you, I sometimes work seven days a week and my daily schedule fluctuates. Because I offer both products and services, there are certain things that I can't delegate to my team. And as much as I love automation and technology, I am old school and thoroughly enjoy responding to clients personally or doing virtual coaching sessions because a phone call isn't enough. With clients on both coasts, I try to accommodate as many business hours as possible. However, I avoid promising anything EOD (end of day) or COB (close of business) because depending on the time zone, that is a recipe for disaster. My commitment to providing my clients with exceptional services and memorable experiences pushes me to be a better businesswoman. It also opens the door for failure.

Paradoxically, we must also accept that failure is often a part of our journey towards success. I can't think of a single entrepreneur who I have worked with or taken on as a client who has not experienced some form of failure. Failure can be defined in numerous ways, but ultimately, I see it as something that did not go as planned—this can be as straightforward as not being awarded a contract to something as complicated as not having the cash flow to pay your business expenses. Regardless of the context, the key is not to stay in that space; instead, learn from your failures, grow from them and push forward.

I am, obviously, not trying to discourage anyone. I just want to add a sprinkle of realism to a larger cultural (and generational) conversation that we seem to be in the midst of. A great way to test this premise is to read the biography of one of your favorite business icons. There is a strong probability that on the road to great success that person encountered failures.

If your business is truly your calling then nothing will stop you—

NOTHING! So, whether you read about the entrepreneurial life, live it, or listen to it, just go into it knowing that your experiences will be as unique and highly configured as you are. Most importantly, hold on to your 'why.' Soon you will find yourself shifting from execution to sustainability.

SUSTAINABILITY

8

MONEY MATTERS: ARE YOU PREPARED TO BE THE BOSS?

"If you really look closely, most overnight successes took a long time."

-Steve Jobs

After launching a business and figuring out how to transition from the ideation phase to the execution phase, it's important not to forget about the stage that often determines whether a company makes it over a sustained period of time and that is sustainability.

Sustainability and longevity are interconnected and for many of us, it is the end goal. Who wants to start something, invest time, energy, and resources into it just for it to dissipate over time or to discover that it's not sustainable? I think it's fair to say that none of us entered the business landscape without some sense of it being a sustainable lifestyle.

Perhaps you are reading this and thinking that you'd love to sustain working for yourself. Or maybe the idea of being the boss resonates with your soul. Well, the next two chapters are all about sustainability.

Throughout this chapter, I am going to share with you how to make sure that you can sustain what you have started and invested so much of your time and energy into. More than anything, as your business grows, as you get more clients and as it becomes more profitable, be clear about the value of your skill set, goods, or product

If you are serious about being an entrepreneur then you need to have a realistic understanding about what you plan to sell. The desire to work for yourself is not enough. You have to have something that is consumable, or that people are willing to pay for.

The best way to determine if there is a market is to conduct research. Have a clear understanding of the demand for your service. This doesn't mean that there isn't a place for creativity and ingenuity—perhaps you cannot find products/goods/services similar to yours because no one else has thought of it.

Don't let that stop you from launching your business, just be realistic. After you have conducted your research, think about your targeted audience.

Point blank, ask yourself: Who wants what I am selling? Remember, in many instances, your locality does not determine the viability of your product. My story is a testimony to this point.

I am located in the Midwest, but almost all of my clients are in California, the New York City area, Atlanta, Detroit, or Chicago. Had I solely focused on where I am located, I probably would still be working for someone else. I wasn't motivated so much by the idea of being an entrepreneur as I was the idea of being free.

Not knowing anything about running a business, I knew that what I did behind the scenes was equally as important as what I did in front of the scenes. As Coach Furcron used to say, "What you do in practice, you will do in the game."

I take that seriously as a business owner. I want to be the best writer and editor that I can be. So, guess what? I write every day and I read every day. Yes, every day. Why? To practice. Some of my writing will appear in front of others, but some won't. Nevertheless, I continue practicing because that is what helps me to improve.

I don't want to get so comfortable or complacent that I don't strive to get better. I tell my clients that I am a player/coach. Many of the techniques and strategies that I recommend to them, I also use.

I want to be that coach who is running layups with her team and not just blowing the whistle and telling others to do it. Therefore, no matter what the enterprise is, you want to be the best at it. There may be 100,000 other vendors who sell t-shirts, so think in terms of what makes you stand out from the crowd.

When it comes to sustainability and being a boss, you are the canary in the mine, so be willing to ask: Why should someone support my business? Is it the quality of your product, the craftsmanship, the style, the ingenuity, the pricing?

For me, I knew that I wanted my customer service and the quality of our services to be cornerstones of our success. Because I had experience working for publishing companies and education systems, I thought in terms of how I could replicate the best parts of those industries' non-proprietary systems and scale them down so that it worked for a company of my size. I added several steps to ensure that we had great quality assurance.

But that wasn't enough. I wanted my clients to feel connected to our brand, so I think of them as members of the Seldon Writing Group village. I jokingly tell them that they are villagers for life unless they decide to run away. This simply means that after the sale, I still try to support them by sharing information about their books, attending their book signings, and staying in touch.

I am not a fan of building a plane while you are flying it. The more you can do to be proactive, the less reactionary you will have to be. There are many of us who have successfully made the transition and here's hoping that you will too!

As the World Evolves, So Must You

Being a boss or the boss has become so ubiquitous that many of us use it without really thinking about what it means or what it requires. One of the most important things about being a boss or a leader is being open to change and to growth.

When I first joined Facebook in 2009, I did so to stay connected to family members, friends, and students. My social media presence was quite capricious and often, to be honest, I went on there just to be nosy—to see who was getting married, having a baby, getting a divorce or all of the above.

This lasted for years until a friend, who is a social media guru, chastised me about being virtually invisible. I told him, "I don't do social media."

At the time, I didn't really see the purpose of having connections with people I didn't actually know. I was content with my 500 friends.

My friend nudged me further and said that I was missing out on a gold mine. He explained how he used his social media presence to introduce potential clients to his work, to create a brand, and to gain greater visibility which he leveraged as a freelance writer and public speaker. "Give it two months," he insisted. I agreed.

It actually took less than a month and I "got it."

Fast forward, and social media has led to some amazing client connections, networking opportunities and international marketing.

So, yes, my friend was right. It is a virtual gold mine if you figure out how to use it to your advantage and I am not talking about algorithms or sponsored ads. I am talking about good old-fashioned human connections—even if they are virtual.

So, what can you do? Try these tips.

Be clear about how much of 'you' you want to share

If you want to get traction on your personal page and that traction is derived from strangers, be very clear and intentional about what you plan to share. Because I brand as a freelance writer who is passionate about writing and social justice issues, I am myopic with my posts.

Occasionally, I may throw in what I ate for dinner last night and I may shout out my partner, but that is rare. I also made some of my old pictures and photo albums private. My rule of thumb when deciding whether or not to post on any platform is: Only share information that you are ok with telling a perfect stranger. As your platform grows, that's who you may end up talking to.

Let's say that you already have a personal Facebook page. As of the time that I am writing this book, Facebook limits personal pages to 5,000 friends. As you watch a significant uptick in people sending you friend requests, it may signal that it is time for you to expand your reach.

You probably don't want to start over and create a public figure page, so I opt to create an additional page—either as your business or a specific product. This will enable you to boost your post and sponsor ads, a valuable resource that I discussed in a previous chapter.

As much as you may not be "into" social media, digitized platforms are here to stay. You don't want to miss opportunities to be impactful and to have an extensive reach.

In some ways Facebook, YouTube, and Instagram have become the trifecta for entrepreneurs who are attempting to expand their visibility and to monetize their brands.

If multiple pages seem unrealistic and you don't want to open up your personal page to others then definitely create a FB page just for your business and invite all of your friends to like and follow it.

Tell people what you do and share
Do your social media connections know that you are a freelancer? When's the last time that you—to the extent that you can—shared some of your work? I underestimated the importance of this at first. It's not enough to just tell people, "I am a _____."

You may have potential clients who are in need of your services and simply sharing that you freelance can lead to transactional relationships. Like I tell my writers, show, don't just tell.

Be consistent in how you use your platforms
One of the most important aspects of social media branding is brand consistency. If you are a freelance videographer, make sure that your social media platforms are aligned with what you do and your area of specialization.

People will start gravitating towards you because they will associate your page with great video products. People will also use what you post as virtual business cards when they tell others about your work.

With Facebook analytics (for non-personal pages), I can gauge the reach of a post, the gender, age-range, and geographic location of the people who follow 2 of my 3 pages. For example, my niche audience on FB are women ages 34 to 55 who live in NYC, Chicago and Houston. 65% of my new clients in 2017 are via Facebook and they fall within this demographic, so I can actually attribute this growth directly to having a social media presence. Had it not been for FB, they probably never would have 'found' me.

Create good content
Good content is like the trailer of a movie that isn't coming out until next year and you've already made plans to see it.

In the social media ecosystem, good content is a status, a post, a tweet, a picture, a caption, a meme or even a hashtag. Links to longer pieces are great, but sometimes, 30 seconds is all that you need. Good content is also like a virtual billboard for your services. I have posted content that has been shared by thousands of people. I also know that my content has reached over a million people. Does this translate into sales? Not necessarily, but it does help with branding and marketing your services.

Venture into new territory
I joined Instagram at the urging of two different clients. "You're missing out, Doc." When I initially thought about Instagram, I thought about scantily clad women and since my modeling days are over, I opted to pass. I really did not understand why it would be advantageous for me from a business standpoint. So, one day, as my client and I were having lunch, I asked him to show me how the hashtags worked.

He showed me a few posts and when he typed in #freelancers, #writers, #authors, # entrepreneurs, and #editors, millions of posts popped up. We clicked on a few and I was pleasantly surprised to see others sharing their written work. I've grown to like Instagram and I primarily use it to share inspirational quotes, cover shots of my clients' books, or a selfie or two.

I also link my company website in my bio and a few links to my blogs. I have made some connections that have resulted in opportunities to freelance. Conversely, Twitter has not panned out as much for me, so I don't actively use it, but it might be right for you.

It is worth noting that because I have watched other people launch and grow businesses using social media platforms, I am drawing from tips that are more process-oriented than personality based. I know my charisma is a factor in some of my success, but these tips are bankable for entrepreneurs anywhere if you give them time.

One other cool thing about posting on multiple social media platforms is that many of them are interconnected, so you really only have to pick one and share from there—there are even apps for that.

Attracting and Sustaining High Value Clients

Although many of us may reduce being a boss to money; it really is about more than that. It is about building trust and rapport with people, including total strangers.

One of my favorite examples of this started with a random email.

An intern for a major music mogul reached out to me to see if I might be interested in consulting for and editing a book project. She said that she'd read some of my work and contacted me via the email address I included in the blogs' bio section. She believed that my writing style was a good fit for her boss and that I would not compromise the integrity of his 'voice'. She concluded the email with her phone number and asked that I call her.

I had to read the email a few times and even after that, I thought it was a phishing scam. So, I Googled her. And there she was with credentials that corroborated the information that she sent me.

Considering that this potential client was someone who I followed when I was younger and who had recently been featured on two different reality TV programs, I knew this was a major opportunity. But, I didn't want to come across as star-struck or like a groupie; therefore, I waited a few days before I called her back.

We had a delightful conversation that felt more like two lost-friends reconnecting than two strangers conversing for the first time. I got so comfortable talking to her that by the time I hung up, I was pretty sure that the gig was not mine. I knew she was vetting me, but I felt like I overshared and she may have walked away with the impression that I was too informal.

A few weeks passed and nada. I continued freelancing and running my company. Then, I received a pleasant text indicating that she had recommended me to her boss' manager and that I should expect a call from his LA team. Within days, his manager called. She proceeded with a series of questions—most of which were about confidentiality, current projects, availability and pricing.

Fast forward through a few more emails and editing samples and I was offered the contract. I worked directly with the client and his team to complete his book project. After the project concluded, we stayed connected and his team has subsequently recommended several other clients.

My client, by definition, is what many would refer to as the coveted high value, or ideal, client. [Please note that I do not subscribe to the idea that any client is low value—all clients are valuable]. High value clients are ones who are industry captains, influencers, celebrities, high-profile, and to be brutally honest, people who can afford higher-end pricing and services. Although, this particular client was my most visible high value client, he was not my first.

Some of you may be thinking, "Why you?" I know it's not a slight to my character or my work; it really is a fair question.

Up until a few months ago, I did not have a website. All of my clients were word-of-mouth or referrals. So, I can't say, in all honesty, that it was a stellar marketing plan or advertisements that lured these clients in and kept them coming back. Instead, I credit my ongoing success to these three things:

Authentic Lead Generation
Like anything, there has to be a starting point or a way to initiate leads or sales with high value clients. Some people will do this via e-newsletters or sharing content via list building. Others will take out digital or print ads. For most of us, this can get to be very expensive and time consuming, but authentic lead generation doesn't have to be.

There are two mediums that are often not leveraged enough—blogging and vlogging [video blogging]. If you write about or speak about topics that you are passionate about that also reflect your business offerings then you are, potentially, going to generate leads. The key is being authentic. I would never recommend blogging or vlogging exclusively for sales, but be mindful that you never know who is reading or watching your work.

Give people a chance to learn more about you and your services without coming across as preachy or engaging in a hard sale. You may offer a service that someone is in need of; as such, always try to include a brief bio and contact information. I am convinced that had the intern not read my blogs, I never would have been on her radar.

Fair Pricing
This one is tricky. You don't want to over/under sell your services. The key is fairness. If you have a high-quality product, people will pay for it. I am not a fan of multi-tier (or scale) fees where certain clients pay one amount and other clients pay another amount for the same, exact service. I charge my clients the same amount, unless someone needs a scholarship because they can't afford my rate. In other words, I don't believe in adding upcharges for high value clients.

Let's be honest, depending on a client's industry and field, his/her yearly salary or net worth may be a matter of public record, so it may be tempting to price gouge, but don't. I actually believe that transparency and fairness in pricing keeps clients coming back and referring their other high value friends and colleagues. It has become an extension of my reputation.

Using Discretion
A Nondisclosure Agreement (NDA) can be your best friend. High value clients value privacy, exclusivity and discretion. In many instances, I am asked to sign an NDA. In other instances, I offer to sign one. Why? In this day and age of social media 'leaks' and an ambiguous line between public and private lives, I want my clients to know that confidentiality governs everything that I do.

Because I am not in the epicenters for my industry (NY and LA); I am a bit of an outlier. High value clients need to know that they can trust me. If having another legally binding document on file reassures them that I am a good fit then "let's do it." Remember, attracting and sustaining high value clients may take some extra time, but be persistent and be real.

Think Like a Client, Process Like a Boss

Content can be used to expand your business's audience, and to strengthen and develop your brand. In other words, your marketing content can also drive leads and sales by appealing to other businesses (B2B is business to business) as well as to customers (B2C is business to customers).

Yet, many small business owners think that these marketing strategies are reserved for larger companies with marketing budgets. Well, think again. Even if you only freelance on the side, you still can benefit from content marketing.

The good news is that you don't need a marketing team to do it and you truly can do-it-yourself. How? By paying attention to and implementing content marketing tactics.

What is Content Marketing?
You may not be comfortable with marketing, but the reality is that with the internet and e-commerce, content marketing has become normative. Revolving around leveraging one's content (written, web-based, digital, and video), it can lead to greater profitability and sustainability. So, how can you capitalize on it?

Think Like a Content Strategist
One of the first things that I recommend is thinking like a content strategist. Do you know your audience? Whether you have two customers or 2,000, think about the demographics, educational levels, genders and even racial and ethnic backgrounds of your current client roster. Now think about other businesses that you currently do business with. What products do they sell? Who are their clientele? Where are they located?

This is an assessment that you can conduct with minimal effort. The most important question is: What does your assessment reveal? There are probably some patterns that emerged—this, in turn, makes up the core demographics of your targeted audience. You may want to start by marketing to this group and then work your way outward. After you identify the clientele patterns that emerge, it's time to put that information to good use.

The next logical question may be: now what? And that boils down to understanding how to leverage three things: being clear about your uniqueness, having value added, and being solution-oriented.

Be Clear about your USP

USP is short for unique selling proposition. USPs are literally everywhere. Think UPS—What can brown do for you? Or Enterprise—Pick Enterprise. We'll pick you up. In both of these examples, the emphasis is placed on what the company can do for its clients – hence the use of the word you.

Short and to the point, the USP encapsulates why a company or freelancer is unique. In light of this, the USP is the why. It is all about making sure that you are telling the right story in a few words, phrases, or a sentence.

For example, when I first started freelancing, I would tell people that I loved helping people make their dreams come true.

Although this was an authentic response, there was nothing unique about it. It took me a while, but eventually, I settled on "Writing Your Dreams into Reality Since 2011" because that is what most of my clients pay me to do—I help them carve out, express, and ultimately turn their writing dreams into realities.

Like many other USPs, I included the word you to clearly earmark that we are service-oriented and I added the establishment date to signify that we've been in existence for a while.

Ready to start? The amount of time that you may initially have to invest in coming up with your USP may seem daunting, especially if content creation, storytelling, and writing are not your areas of expertise. The good news is that you know your story better than anyone else.

Understand Value Added B2B Marketing

If you want to increase your volume and the number of B2B customers that you have then think about what you have to offer that would lead to "value added" for that business—in other words, what do you bring that a potential competitor cannot.

Are you a SME—subject matter expert? Do you have numerous years of experience? Do you have a clientele roster that reflects the depth and breadth of your ability? These are tangible and commodifiable assets that many businesses are willing to pay [more] for. However, if you do not leverage these benefits in the verbiage of your content marketing then how will they know?

I have found that businesses ranging from small business to Fortune 100 companies are more willing to use your services if your marketing clearly reflects the value added that you bring to a project.

Embrace Solution-Oriented B2C Marketing
What value added is to B2B is what solution-oriented is to B2C. Specifically, if your goal is to increase your B2C customers then value added may not be as important, but fulfilling a specific need is. Most successful freelance careers are launched because a freelancer saw a need and was able to fill it with a particular product, good, or service.

Often B2C marketing is easier for entrepreneurs. With B2C marketing, you are dealing with individuals who have the autonomy to make decisions. The key to standing out from the competition is being clear about the gap or the problem that your services or products solve.

And, once again, this approach all begins with the content that you use to consistently convey your messaging.

So, whether you have been using these strategies or you plan to start, remember that the genesis of any content marketing process starts with you.

Why Self-Funding Your Own Business at This Stage May Not be the Best Idea

Did you know that if you have a business then you may be able to secure funding without having to leverage your own personal credit?

Because a freelancer's revenue or income may fluctuate from month-to-month or project to project, it is sometimes difficult to get access to cash from traditional lending sources like banks. For many of us, the traditional model of applying for a secured bank loan or line of credit just won't work because on paper, we may be seen as high risk.

So, what can you do when you're at the point when bootstrapping is no longer a viable option or you need to generate additional revenue but you don't want to continue pulling from your own personal resources or you don't want your personal credit to be the determining factor in securing funds? You may want to consider establishing business credit.

What is business credit?
Unlike personal credit which is connected to your SSN, business credit is credit that revolves around the health and history of your business as it relates to your business' ability to borrow and pay back money. Logically, if your business has never borrowed money then how can you demonstrate a history of credit worthiness? Well, you can't.

And that's why business credit is not as easy to secure as personal credit. Think about entrepreneurs who would benefit from a corporate credit card. Large corporations like Dell, Target, and COSTCO will want you to demonstrate or prove that your business is credit worthy before issuing a business credit card, regardless of your income, earning potential, or personal credit score.

Now, I am far from an expert, but here's what I have uncovered as I have tried to figure out if this is the best next step for my company (which was born out of freelancing).

Get your numbers ready.
You will need an EIN and DUNS number. DUNS is used to monitor your company's credit score.

Establish NET 30 vendor lines of credit.
Think of the supplies that you use like paper, ink cartridges, toilet paper, and envelopes. Rather than directly purchasing these items from a big box store or a national retailer, you may want to consider purchasing them from a company that is willing to give you 30-day net in business credit.

This allows you to establish credit history by providing your EIN; the retailer establishes a trade line in your company's name; they supply the product to you and you pay for it. According to creditsuite.com, it's important to try to establish at least 5 vendor lines of credit.

"You need to have a total of at least five (5) Net 30 day pay accounts reporting... Pay your Net 30 vendor accounts in full and on time. You must be patient and allow time for the vendors' reporting cycles to get into the reporting systems. It typically takes 3 cycles of "Net" accounts reporting to build credit scores."

Good credit is the objective.
The key is that you want to pay your balance within the specified time-the sooner, the better. If you don't pay within the specified timeframe, this can have the opposite effect of what you want and you will end up establishing a negative credit history which defeats the purpose.

Your trade lines and payment history will get reported as a part of your company's credit history. If you are intentional about building up your net 30 trade lines, before you know it, you will be positioned to get additional lines of credit. With this credit, you don't have to have as much cash flow during those periods when business may be slower than you anticipated.

Over time, you can leverage your credit to secure a traditional loan, get business credit cards, and establish your business credit worthiness.

Is it worth it?
Now, for some of us, this may sound like jumping through hoops

with high heels on during a thunderstorm. The verdict is still out for me, but I know people who have had great success using this to take some of the financial pressure off.

So, I strongly encourage you to do additional research and make an informed decision to determine if obtaining business credit is best for you.

Why You Should Use Incentive Programs

Restaurants, airline companies, grocery stores, and department stores have been successfully incentivizing people for years. Here's how it works: Imagine that there are two grocery stores that carry similar products. The quality of the products and the customer service are comparable. They are both of equal distance from your home. One will give you 5% off of your total purchase and one will not.

Most of us would probably patronize the store that offers the incentive. Why? If you know that you are going to gain value from something or you are going to get a greater return on your investment then you will probably gravitate towards the provider that rewards you. Look at your key ring: Does this sound familiar?

When you think about incentives, you may not think about using them for your freelancing business, but maybe you should. As consumers, it's great feeling appreciated and valued. When a company recognizes your value and rewards you for your loyalty, it's an added incentive to patronize them. The same just might apply with your clients.

Whether it's just you, or you and a handful of employees, here are three simple and cost-effective ways that you can incentivize clients.

Service Giveaways

How many cups, pens, and promotional bags do you have? If you are like me, you have acquired quite a few over the years. Although these are great for trade shows and in-store freebies, they may not work as well for entrepreneurs. This is why you may want to consider what I call service giveaways.

Service giveaways are pretty straightforward. You incentivize clients by offering them an additional service (with an actual cash value) for free or at a reduced rate. This isn't about branding or about marketing, it's about attracting new clients and rewarding returning ones. Therefore, the key is coming up with something that will add value for your client.

Because of this, consider adding your giveaway service to a service that you are already providing. For example, if you are a photographer, you may add a free head shot photo shoot once a client has contracted for over $1500.00 in services. This serves as an incentive for the client. He/she may be more inclined to come back to you for future services knowing that there is something extra in it for him/her, especially if the incentive has real-world value.

Membership Rewards

Unlike the service giveaways, a membership rewards program is not tied to the frequency and/or amount of money that a client spends with you. Membership focuses more on intangibles than actual cash value. If you are old enough, think about the Members Only jackets commercials. The commercial's tagline was brilliant: "Membership has its privileges." Everyone I went to school with wanted a jacket, not because they were of a certain quality or particularly stylish, but because they were marketed as being exclusive.

The same psychology works with membership programs. Only members of a rewards program get access to the information or special invites. Yes, it has value because information has value, but unlike giving away a service, you are offering access to information, resources, or events that are exclusive to members only. For example, a freelance accountant may offer a webinar for 1099 employees or create an online seminar that is restricted to his/her rewards members—faithful clients.

Sending out valuable information via email about your field or industry can also add to the value of a client being a member of the group. The incentive is exclusivity; your clients have access to something that is not readily available to the public. And because you have built relationships with them, it gives them greater access to your expertise, creativity, and knowledge.

Finder's Fee

Think about how often you have referred someone or someone has referred you. It happens quite frequently. Many entrepreneurs thrive off of 'word of mouth' referrals. What if there were an extra incentive for your clients to recommend you? Have you thought about creating a Finder's Fee program?

A Finder's Fee is also, sometimes, referred to as an affiliate fee. Its premise is logical. If you are under contract with someone to serve as an affiliate and that person recommends your services and the person who was recommended becomes a client then the recommender receives a fee (typically a percentage) for generating the new contract. For example, if you are a graphic designer, you may have a Finder's Fee that stipulates that you will pay someone 15% for every new and fully executed contract over $2,000.00 that the affiliate generates.

Because the affiliate is the catalyst for the new client, you are paying him/her for his/her services. As simple as this may seem, I would not recommend using this program without consulting legal counsel and a CPA. There are both tax and legal implications.
Why would this appeal to a freelancer? There's only so much marketing that you can do. Our clients are potential walking billboards for our services.

If implemented effectively, this can generate numerous new clients, especially if you have clients who have large networks and whose endorsements/referrals can lead to tangible results.

The Value of Loyal Clients
In working with new business owners, one of their greatest concerns is building up their clientele. Whether you've been freelancing for a few months or several years, most of us would love to have a consistent and faithful client base that not only keeps coming back, but recommends us to others. This can lead to long term success and viability.

Overhead vs. Profitability

Some people get baby fever; I, occasionally, get office fever. A dear friend recently leased a 5,000-square-foot space, one floor of a multi-story building. As he was giving me a tour, my eyes bulged with excitement as I thought about all of the wonderful things that I would do if it were my space. I envisioned where our (non-existent) receptionist would sit, where we would encase all of our clients' books, and where I would set up working spaces for our freelance writers and editors.

And then, almost on cue, he told me about his monthly rent. I went from thoughts of marigold walls and laptop portals to financial fatigue. It was a reality check—a reality check that I needed about how much overhead can impact one's bottom line.

Workspaces of the future
Although there is prestige that comes with having a brick-and-mortar space, and some businesses require it, it is not necessary for many of us. When you factor in rent/mortgage, additional insurance, monthly utilities, wi-fi, parking, and other fees, having a traditional office can get to be very expensive.

For those reasons, many of us opt to go the less traditional, yet the increasingly more popular routes of co-working or remote work. A friend and Freelancer's Union member, Robert McGrath, will soon publish a book that takes a deep dive into co-working, What is Co-Working? I refer you to his book for a more nuanced discussion, but for now, here are some things to consider about keeping your overhead low:

Do you really need an office?
Because most of the work that I do is digital or virtual, it is rare that I have to physically meet with people. Yet, I have a brick and mortar office space because there are occasions when clients prefer to meet in-person.

For those of you who find that you are in front of a laptop more than you are sitting in front of a stationary desk, taking on the fiscal overhead of a designated office space is probably not worth it. Instead, places like Starbucks, coffee houses, public libraries, or even restaurants may be much cheaper, or free, alternatives.

Unfortunately, Starbucks was in the news for an incident of blatant racism that occurred at one of its Philly locations. After the incident, I thought about how, over the years, I have used Starbucks to meet clients and potential clients. The ambiance is great, the seating is comfortable, there is often convenient parking and free wi-fi. I am not a coffee drinker, so I make a point of buying a bottle of water. The $2.99 that I pay for the water pales in comparison to what I would pay to either lease or rent something similar.

The variables of the nomadic office
Conversely, the disadvantage of using places like a Starbucks, or an independently owned coffee shop, is that there are many variables that you cannot control, including the noise level, the physical capacity, and the level of privacy that you will be afforded. If these things are deal breakers or interfere with your ability to perform your services, then you may need your own designated space. If so, consider a co-working facility or renting a singular office or desk as opposed to renting an entire office suite or an office building.

When seeking out spaces, be realistic about what you can afford. Look at your last year's earnings and your projections for the current year and the next year. If anything changes in your forecast, will you still have enough money to cover your monthly expenses? Most traditional office spaces will make you sign a six-month to year-long lease. Because your personal credit history may be used during the application process, you definitely don't want to take on more than you can afford.

This leads to the next question that I want you to consider.

Will a virtual presence be just as effective?
My first webinar was awkward. In my previous professional lives, I'd grown accustomed to sitting around a large conference table or in mid-sized auditoriums. I could literally see, feel, and touch my colleagues if I so desired.

So, shifting to virtual sessions took some getting used to. Initially, I had difficulty figuring out simple things like how to mute attendees or how to ensure that the volume was appropriate. I even had a meeting where someone was upside down.

Honestly, going from in-person meetings to shared screens and computer cameras may be an adjustment, but it is worth it, especially if you are trying to keep your overhead low. There are several platforms that you can use. I strongly advise that you research which one is the best fit for you. My favorite, because of ease of use, is Zoom.

For less than $40.00 a month, I can stay connected to my team of independent contractors, most of whom do not live in my city. I can also meet with clients at times that are convenient for them—this is particularly advantageous if your clients live in different time zones. Most importantly, having the capacity to engage with clients virtually gives you an additional option for how you deliver your services. This may not work for all entrepreneurs, but if it fits within the scope of your work, definitely give it a try!

The bottom line
If you really want to increase your cash flow and your profit margins, pay particular attention to where and how you are spending your money. Re-occurring costs tend to be the costliest because they add up over a sustained period of time.

To determine if an overhead cost is worth it, conduct a cost-benefit analysis. This can be as simple as stepping back and asking: Do I really need to do this? Your answer to this question can be the starting point for keeping your overhead low and your profit margins higher.

To Collaborate or Not

It may appear in the form of an email, an inbox or a DM on social media. The message typically starts benign enough with a friendly introduction, a brief description and then an amazing pitch about why you need to partner or do business with the sender. Some of these are scams; some are phishing expeditions; some are templates, but some may actually be legitimate opportunities to enter into a mutually beneficial relationship.

I have been approached enough in the last 7 years that I now have a non-scientific and non-empirical approach for determining if I delete, mark as junk, block, reply or partner. Because acronyms help us to remember important information, I call it: M.O.S. It is a simple and effective way to determine if potentially going into business with someone or partnering with him/her is a good idea.

Mission Alignment or Mission Adrift

Whether it is publicly stated, written down, or just carried in our hearts, we all tend to have a mission—or something that guides our actions, decisions, and relationships. When vetting potential business partners, it is worth the time to conduct a little research. What is this person/company's mission? Does it align with yours?

If you partner with someone whose mission conflicts with yours or leads to an area of either business or personal ambiguity then it will affect the partnership. For example, if your goal is to enter into a partnership for altruistic purposes and the other person is looking strictly at the bottom line, you will probably clash at some point. The key is avoiding that clash.

In his book *Good to Great: Why Some Companies Make the Leap and Others Don't*, Jim Collins uses the analogy of having the right people on your bus. In an article derived from the book, he writes:

> "You are a bus driver. The bus, your company, is at a standstill, and it's your job to get it going. You have to decide where you're going, how you're going to get there, and who's going with you.
>
> Most people assume that the great bus drivers (read: business leaders) immediately start the journey by announcing to the

people on the bus where they're going—by setting a new direction or by articulating a fresh corporate vision.

In fact, leaders of companies that go from good to great start not with "where" but with "who." They start by getting the right people on the bus, the wrong people off the bus, and the right people in the right seats. And they stick with that discipline—first the people, then the direction—no matter how dire the circumstances."

https://www.jimcollins.com/article_topics/articles/good-to-great.html

If you are heading north and another passenger wants to head south, you will not reach the same destination. Someone will have to get off of the bus and hopefully that someone will not be you. Thankfully this is preventable which leads to my next step.

Opportunity or Opportunist

The right opportunity can serve as a launching pad that introduces our work to new clients and presents us with new opportunities to grow and expand our business. Who does not want this?

The problem is that not all opportunities are the right ones or the right ones at the right time. Opportunists tend to prey on people who may be vulnerable or susceptible to the right words sprinkled with just a pinch of charisma. Even the most guarded and intelligent people can get caught in an opportunist's net. As with most of the things on the list, it is important that you listen with your ears, process with your brain, and follow your gut.

Intuition is not given the credit that it deserves in the business world—perhaps because it is not quantifiable—none the less, there are typically flags that go up when dealing with an opportunist and the largest one revolves around execution and follow-through. What is this person's track record? Have they done for others what they claim that they will do for you?

Ask for data, documentation, referrals, recommendations. And most important, do due diligence. Of course, not everyone has a digital imprint, but most people do. Learn as much as you can, especially considering that business partnerships require the exchange of money, time, and precious resources.

Social Media Real or Really Real

I have a mercurial relationship with social media. On one hand, I love it and I am thankful for how it has led to greater visibility for my work and my brand. On the other hand, it irks me. Actually, not so much "it", but the people who use it to create facades or veneers.

Because of the nature of my work, I meet people who are literally from all walks of life. This has led to some amazing partnerships and some worthwhile partnerships. It has also taught me a valuable lesson about people who profess one thing on social media, but whose real lives are mismatched.

Let's be honest: Anyone can create a fabulous life, or business, on social media. Some eye-catching photographs, eloquently worded posts and dynamically shot video footage can give the impression of a time-tested, well-established business. But, is it really real?

In many instances, yes, it is. People have legitimate business and they simply use social media as a marketing tool to further expose their work. However, there are also people who use those social media businesses as virtual shells—empty shells. As such, when it comes to potentially partnering with someone who you have met in a virtual space, I highly recommend that you don't allow the fast-pace or real-time expediency of social media to prevent you from taking your time.

You may want to Google the person or start following them on social media, especially if they have a business page. Ask for a website address, but keep in mind that some legitimate businesses do not have them. Lastly, if you feel comfortable, coordinate a phone call or a virtual meeting (Zoom.com has a free option). Try to learn as much as you can. And again, trust your gut. If a partnership is worth it, the other person should understand why you are treating the opportunity as if it is a marathon and not a sprint.

Now, this binary approach is not for everyone nor is it fool-proof. However, it has helped me save valuable time and energy when dealing with potential business partners and co-collaborators.

It's Not Just About Money

Obviously, a critical component of sustainability is profitability. However, I want you to also consider a measurement of success that most entrepreneurs share—philanthropy. You don't have to be a multi-million-dollar operation to give back.

Throughout my professional career, I worked for institutions and colleges that were deeply vested in philanthropic work. This would range from having the option of having money withheld from our bi-weekly paychecks for United Way to adopting a school in a foreign country.

Since transitioning from working for someone else to working for myself, philanthropy has taken on a different meaning. I no longer have the ease of showing up for an event on behalf of my employer or checking off a box for my HR representative. Now, I have to be more intentional and deliberate in cultivating relationships with organizations that advocate for causes that I believe in. In light of this, I have uncovered that giving back is not only doable, but quite enjoyable. Here are 5 ways that you too can be philanthropic as a business owner:

Volunteer
One of the reasons that I did not engage in that much philanthropic work when I first started freelancing was because I had grown so accustomed to volunteering in groups, that I did not even know where to begin. Now, I realize that Meetups and virtual communities are great ways to mobilize other entrepreneurs to engage in service, especially if that service is hands-on. Depending on where you live, some community organizations prefer if groups volunteer and they may not accept or have a need for a single volunteer. So, reach out to

a fellow freelancer and see if it's feasible for you to volunteer together.

Adopt a Not-for-Profit or Community Group
In 2018, Seldon Writing Group, LLC adopted a small, independent transitional housing facility called Dayspring Center. By adopt, I simply mean that my we volunteer there throughout the year. As much as I wish I could whip out an extra-large check with many zeroes on it, that's not feasible right now. But what is feasible is engaging in sweat equity, including painting, helping to organize supplies, serving food, and doing some light maintenance work. As of 2019, we have implemented the Seldon Writing Group Day of Service with the goal of volunteering once a quarter.

Dedicate Your Anniversary or Birthday to a Cause
Social media, and Facebook in particular, has made it much easier to engage in philanthropic causes. Facebook will allow you to share your cause with your FB friends, and make donating as simple as clicking a button. It will also keep people updated about how well you are doing in reaching your monetary goal. It is an easy way to raise funds for an organization that you believe in. The cool thing is that you can use your birthday (or freelancing anniversary) as the occasion, so instead of gifts and well wishes, people can donate on your behalf.

Donate your Unused Supplies
If you look around your work space, there is a strong possibility that you have a box, shelf, or file cabinet full of 'things' that you are no longer using. While we may not give much thought to these items, there are people within our communities who truly can be blessed by our excess. Shelters for women, places of worship, schools in impoverished areas, and food pantries are places that may gladly accept your donations. Because I believe that all people should be treated with compassion, make sure that you are not getting rid of junk or things that are no longer functional. Before I donate, I ask: Would I want this?

Tutor or Volunteer at a School
If you have paid attention to the state of our K-12 educational

systems then you know that many of our students are in great need of positive adult contact and role modeling. One way that entrepreneurs can give back is by sharing our skill sets with younger children. Skills that may come naturally to us—accounting, writing, speaking, drawing, debating, taking pictures—may be skills or areas that a child needs extra support in.

Do note that gone are the days when you can just pop up at a school, so make sure that you call to find out what is required before you can start volunteering. Many school districts now require background checks and even fingerprinting. There may be a lapse in time between when you express interest in volunteering and when you can actually start, so be patient. The wait is worth the joy you will see in a child's eyes when you help her pronounce a difficult word or show him how to work through the steps for a difficult math problem.

Marian Wright Edelman is credited with saying, "Service is the rent we pay for being. It is the very purpose of life, and not something you do in your spare time." I have found that pouring into my community and engaging in service has enhanced my life tremendously. In fact, it has made me a better freelancer, business owner, and most importantly, a better human being.

Peace of Mind

Since I started my business, there have been numerous studies that have explored the appeal of self-employment. Many of these have focused on tangibles such as work/life balance and the financial rewards that one can enjoy being self-employed. But a recent study caught my attention because it didn't simply replicate the same narrative, it captured what so many of us know to be true: Self-employment can also lead to happiness.

Recently published in the journal *Work, Employment and Society*, the study was conducted by professors who are affiliated with the University of Exeter and the University of Sheffield. The survey size of 5,000 workers is noteworthy, as well as the fact that respondents were from all across the globe, including the United Kingdom, the

United States, Australia, and New Zealand.

The participants were from several sectors in the workplace. They either worked in various traditional roles, including non-managerial, supervisory, senior management, and directorship positions, or they were self-employed in fields and industries including consulting, real estate, insurance, and financial services.

The Results

According to the findings, people who are self-employed tend to be the most engaged; they have numerous opportunities to be innovative; they can set and meet high expectations; and they are more inclined to achieve challenging goals when compared to their peers.

One of the lead researchers, Ilke Inceoglu, indicated that, "Being engaged in their jobs makes people feel [energized] and pleased with their own contribution. Measuring how engaged people are in their work is therefore a really useful way to gauge their wellbeing and shows we must move beyond just looking at job satisfaction."

Fellow lead researcher Peter Warr, from the University of Sheffield, noted that, "Professional workers who are self-employed really value the autonomy they have. They have the freedom to innovate, express their own views, have influence beyond their own role and compete with other companies and people. They really get to use their own expertise, so don't seem to mind working long hours. They can find meeting high standards really fulfilling."

The researchers equate these metrics to being indicators of happiness; hence, they drew the conclusion that when compared to their peers who are employed, self-employed individuals are the happiest.

Changing the narrative about the benefits of self-employment

Not that we needed convincing, but it is always an added bonus when research corroborates what many of us already know: There are numerous, sometimes intangible, perks to being self-employed.

For those of us who have been self-employed for a while, it is probably fair to say that we often set standards that are much higher than those that were once set for us by others. Meeting or exceeding those standards often motivates us and drives us more than a paycheck. In turn, many of us are willing to endure the feast-or-famine conundrum if it means that we don't have to work for someone else.

In other words, there is more to work than just productivity and a paycheck. This is especially true for those of us who have not been self-employed our entire adult lives. When we focus on self-employment exclusively through the lenses of output, material or financial gain, we miss an opportunity to discuss some of the intangibles that keep millions of us self-employed. They are rewards that, often, have little to do with monetary gain, status or cultural capital.

Intangible value
For example, there is something intrinsically valuable about doing your absolute best or beating a personal record that can't quite translate into zeroes on a paycheck. And, as most of us know, there is nothing quite like working on a task or project and engaging with a client who is happy with our work.

And that is why this study, with global implications, is so important. It offers another layer of context that is worth exploring when we engage in larger conversations about the personal and societal benefits of having a thriving self-employed sector. For many of us who are self-employed, simply getting paid to do something, or to perform a service, is not the primary indicator of our happiness; and, hopefully, this study will provide an opportunity for us to continue to discuss both the tangible and intangible benefits of self-employment.

9

MAKING SUSTAINABILITY A CORNERSTONE OF YOUR BUSINESS

The busy man is never wise and the wise man is never busy.

-Lin Yutang

"What will you do for retirement?"

"I'll be just fine. I'm doing something that I love, so retirement is not an issue. In fact, I really don't plan on retiring. I'll just keep writing until I can't write anymore."

I have to admit that the first time someone asked me about retirement, I didn't give it much thought. With two parents who retired from traditional jobs that either included a 401K or a pension, I'd only understood retirement through the vantage point of two people who worked for others their entire adult lives. At the time, I didn't personally know anyone who had retired from being self-employed or from owning a business.

And since I was in my thirties and freelancing was a second career, it didn't seem like a pressing question at the time. Now that I have more years of experience, I return to the question: What about the future?

This question also came back up when I recently talked with a young lady, in her late thirties, who is thinking about freelancing full-time. After we discussed all of the benefits, we had a tough conversation about money. We talked about feast or famine, we talked about surplus and shortfalls, and we talked about the million-dollar question that lingered throughout our discussion: What about the future?

I shared with her that as a new birthday approaches and I inch closer to retirement age, I am starting to give a lot more thought to life after freelancing: specifically, will I have enough saved to enjoy my golden years?

It's human nature to wonder about one's future. There are so many variables that we can't control and this can lead to angst and fretting. It can also lead to regrets and doubts. Couple those concerns with an ever-changing political climate and global economic infrastructure and the thought of the future, especially one's long-term financial forecast, may be daunting.

But, as I shared with her, it doesn't have to be.

One's preparation doesn't have to be complicated. Like many of us, I am familiar with 401Ks, stocks, bonds, real estate and mutual funds. What I am still learning about is the best way to prepare for the days when contracts aren't coming in or I am no longer able to, or don't have the desire to, write. As much as entrepreneurship works for me now, it may not look the same in my sixties and seventies.

One of the worst things imaginable is that some of us may regret the decision to work for ourselves when we are older because we are ill-equipped to truly enjoy the fruits of our labor. The reality is that whether you are 20 or 59 years old, we all need to be prepared, especially with potential reiterations of social security and medical insurance over the next few decades.

Because of this, it's important to have a working understanding of what you can do now to prepare for later. Although there are several retirement options that you can explore, I want to explore a route called SEP that may be helpful for the overwhelming majority of us who fall into one of the following categories: 1) self-employed, 2) freelancer "on the side," or 3) small business owner.

SEP (Simplified Employee Pension)
According to the IRS, "A Simplified Employee Pension (SEP) plan provides business owners with a simplified method to contribute toward their employees' retirement as well as their own retirement savings. Contributions are made to an Individual Retirement Account or Annuity (IRA) set up for each plan participant (a SEP-IRA)."

SEPs are similar in scope to a traditional IRA. You can set up a SEP account for yourself as well as for your employees, if you have any. SEPs are particularly beneficial if you are a sole proprietor, if you still work (and you have other retirement accounts) and freelance on the side, or if you own an LLC and you want to contribute to your contractors' retirement.

How to apply for a SEP
The application process is user-friendly and self-employed fillers can open one up and fund it up until the tax deadline for their business. To get the process started, complete the Form 5305-SEP or the Simplified Employee Pension: Individual Retirement Accounts Contribution Agreement. You can set up a SEP account through banks, insurance agencies, or brokerage firms.

Another benefit of a SEP, especially for second career entrepreneurs, is that you can open a SEP account even if you have a 401K that you have rolled over from a previous employer. To learn even more about SEPs, check out this link: https://www.irs.gov/retirement-plans/plan-sponsor/simplified-employee-pension-plan-sep

The most important takeaway is to plan for your future today. Whether it is a SEP or some other pathway, decide what is the best option for you. The key thing is that you are thinking about the future *now* and protecting those things that you have worked so hard to acquire. If doing it yourself is not ideal, it is worth noting that a financial advisor, wealth management specialist or a CPA may be of great value as you take a deeper dive to explore your options and decide what's best for you.

Other Options for Building Up Your Reserves and Saving for Retirement and Rainy Days

There are certain infrastructures that all of us can put in to place that will lead towards a more sustainable trajectory.

Have multiple-months reserved

If there is a canary in the mine, it is often money. Realistically, we need it and too often, it is the lack of steady income or enough income that deters entrepreneurs from pushing through the tough times. Even for those entrepreneurs who have enjoyed financial stability, it is still important to have a cushion. Whether you refer to this as a savings, rainy day fund, or reserves, the premise is the same—be prepared.

The nature of being an entrepreneur is that some months will be better. Even if your average monthly income is predictable, it's probably never the same. Just as you have insurance for your home, car, life, business, and your health, it's important to have some built-in insurance that if a contract falls through, a client leaves you, or you need to take an unplanned leave, this does not become the catalyst for you to quit freelancing. Ideally, try to put away for multiple months—3, 6, or 9—based upon what your monthly expenses are.

Be willing to Evolve

There was a time when I edited by pen then I started using Word and the track changes function. I slowly started editing PDFs and now many of my clients prefer that their documents are edited using Google docs. This all changed over a relatively short period of time. Although I miss my red pen, I had to adjust or risk being left behind.

In fact, I cannot think of a single industry that has not, or does not, change in some capacity. As entrepreneurs, we have to be willing to evolve. Sometimes this involves integrating new technology or software into our lives. In other instances, it is necessary that we attend conferences, workshops, or even online courses.

We can't be so stuck in our way of doing something or 'how things used to be' that we don't grow, even if that growth leads to growing pains. Does this mean that we should forsake best practices for some new gadget just because it is new? Absolutely not! But, it does mean that if we want to compete, which ultimately leads to greater sustainability, we need to pivot when necessary.

Maintain your Stamina—A few years ago, I worked out at the gym 3 to 4 times a week. As a former athlete, I understood that there would be days when I just didn't want to work out, but I conditioned myself to go and finish, even when I didn't feel like it. As I built up my stamina, working out became such a steady part of my life that it was unusual for me not to go.

In some ways, being a business owner is just like this. Whereas we often think of stamina as a sustained physical effort, it is worth noting that stamina can also mean a sustained mental effort. Our mentality towards something will also determine how we react to it. If entrepreneurship is something that you are committed to doing long term, be willing to put in the work, not just physically, but mentally as well.

Sustainability, or the ability to continue at a certain level, is a realistic outcome for many of us. Yet, it is not uncommon for some of us to give up during this stage, not because we don't love it and not because we are experiencing fatigue, but because we find that either the revenue isn't there, our clientele has plateaued, or the market is over saturated. All of these potential hurdles are realistic, but they are just that—hurdles, not impenetrable fortresses.

Are You Ready for Elevation?

Now that we have covered the financial aspect of sustainability, it is important to discuss a different form of readiness. Sometimes the very thing that we desire is the thing that we are not prepared for. If your desire is to have your product on every shelf at Target, have you thought about inventory, distribution, and warehousing? If your dream is to become a YouTube influencer, have you thought about how this will affect your family? If you desire to become an *American Idol*, have you factored in how much of your private life will become public?

I am not sharing these examples to be discouraging or disparaging; I am sharing them to emphasize that we need to think about the implications of elevation and growth so that we can be prepared.

For a brief period, I engaged in a couple of podcasts and YouTube interviews. Some of them were very popular and had over 100,000 views. At the time, I was ambivalent about whether or not I wanted to be in front of the camera. As the expectations grew, I felt as if it was pulling me away from my writing. At that moment, I made the decision to pivot away from these opportunities because I was not prepared to integrate them into my already robust life.

Whether you are just starting out or you have been in business for a while, ask yourself: Are you ready for the future?

As a recent article in *Forbes* argues, the days of working hard for one company and retiring are over. In the new economy, diversification will lead the way. So how do you prepare?

Conduct a self-inventory to determine your level of mastery and proficiency in certain skill sets
Personally, I love writing and editing. But I have some writer friends who despise editing, and some editor friends who don't consider themselves good writers. I find that diversification is incredibly helpful as a freelancer, but you cannot really decide what is going to work best for you if you don't take the time to step back and conduct an honest assessment about what you are good at doing.

Do a little research
Determine what's hot in your field or industry. Is this a trend or is it something that is sustainable? If it is sustainable, you may want to

invest your time, energy, and resources into learning more, especially if it can lead to a tangible return on your investment. For example, I am noticing more and more opportunities for freelance writers who have experience writing for the business and tech industries. Traditionally, these jobs were only viable for those with a background in technical writing.

However, as the market expands, I strongly recommend that freelance writers become acquainted with aspects of technical writing. As our society becomes more technologically savvy and more industries need people to translate their goods and services into lay terms then there is a strong possibility that this skill set will continue to be in high demand.

Invest in yourself
I never imagined that at this stage in my life, I'd still be interested in taking classes. Although I am not physically stepping into a classroom space, I am a student again. I find myself reading articles and books, watching Podcasts and YouTube videos, and seeking out the counsel of other writers and entrepreneurs who I respect and trust. If this method doesn't work for you, you may want to consider taking an online course and/or taking a class at a local college or university.

This can make the difference between stumbling in the dark and entering a room with a light that is already on. My business coach and spiritual coach have helped me stay focused and avoid many of the pitfalls that often occur when entering into a second career. I, in turn, am a writing coach.

The overwhelming majority of my clients are in their 30s, 40s, and 50s. Many of them realize that their professional and personal success hinges on their ability to effectively communicate, especially in their writing. Remember, your measurable growth is a return on your investment and if it means that you are better positioned to gain traction as a freelancer then why not?

The great news is that the freelancing ecosystem is one that welcomes ingenuity, creativity, and professionalism. Some of the decisions that you make now will determine how well you will be able to compete in this new economy.

And, as with many things, our outcomes and outputs are often determined by an initial investment of our time, energy, and resources.

Your Life's Work, Your Legacy: Is it Time To Write that Book?

One of our clients is 61 and another one is 80. Like most of the authors that my company works with, they both have decided to share a wealth of expertise with others by writing full-length books. We also have a range of clients in their 20s, 30s, 40s, and 50s—many of whom are business owners. Why might they and someone like you, consider writing a book?

There is a growing population of people who are entering into the realm of book writing. Ranging from clinicians and retired professors to social media influencers and self-taught entrepreneurs, book writing is no longer reserved for those who have formal training in writing or who have literary agents or large publishing presses chasing them down and offering them 6 figure advances.

Book writing now belongs to the people, as it should. And it is one of the reasons why I strongly encourage people to tell their stories or to share their expertise even if writing is not in their wheelhouse. And as most people who have worked with me can attest, my objective isn't to convert people into clients; instead, it is to preserve the powerful art of storytelling, especially in this day and age of quick tweets and IG posts.

With advances in self-publishing, writing has become more egalitarian which means that everyone reading this book has access to platforms that will publish his/her work. So, you may be thinking: *Me? Write a book? Why? How?*

You have something of value to say, so make the time
One of the best ways to preserve one's cultural milieu or to share

one's expertise or to introduce one's ideas and kernels of wisdom to others, especially to complete strangers, is through words.

Unless you plan to hire a ghost writer, the value you place on what you have to say is by far one of the most important factors in determining whether or not you complete your manuscript. Your average 200-page book is 50,000 words. If you factor in life's responsibilities, it is important that you are realistic about how much time you can consistently dedicate to the writing process.

The antidote to this is being proactive. Realistically, sketch out a writing schedule and give it the same importance and consideration that you would a critical business or personnel endeavor. There is a strong possibility that you already have the baseline content: PowerPoint presentations, blogs, personal notes, best practices material, manuals, etc. This content can be the springboard for a book.

Lastly, it is also helpful if you have an accountability partner who can check in to make sure that you are actually writing and staying on task. Create realistic benchmarks, such as a chapter per month. If you are committed to the process and build in these safety nets, you will have the stamina to write a full-length book.

There is an audience for your work
As you think about your book idea and concept, you want to ask: Who am I writing this text for? Beyond your immediate circle of family members, friends, and peers, are you writing about a topic that potential strangers want to read?

It is not vain to think that your narrative (fiction or non-fiction) is worthy of an audience. I firmly believe that most of us are gifted with stories. Our life experiences, expressed through our stories, make us human. Because of this, you would probably be amazed by the diverse book topics and audiences that exist.

If you are really curious, check out the books section on Amazon.com. Yes, some of these authors are professional writers, but many of them are not. Some of the books are about serious topics and required years of research and others are lighter hearted. (And some people even use pseudonyms, so if you want to write, but under a pen name, go for it!)

Self-publishing has changed book writing
For better or for worse, self-publishing has changed how we think about authorship There was a time when publishing a book was an elitist endeavor reserved for professional writers, poets, historians and those who were deemed worthy of the resources and marketing budget of a major publishing company. Often the criteria for publishing was based on the bottom line: Can this person write a profitable book?

The pendulum has swung and although this is still an important question, there are those who have decided to write books not as business endeavors, but because they want to preserve their ideas for posterity's sake or their thoughts may be too controversial for mainstream presses or their topic may only be of interest to a niche audience. Regardless of the impetus, self-publishing, also known as print on demand, has opened doors that were once closed to many.

Keep in mind that with the amount of stamina, time, creative energy, and financial resources (e.g. editing, typesetting, and book covers) that go into writing a book, it is important that you don't enter into the space without having a clear sense of what you are getting into. However, you will probably find that book writing can be a deeply rewarding experience and it's worth the sacrifice.

Because writing is a deeply personal endeavor, only you can decide if you are ready to write a book. If so, happy writing!

Soft Skills that Don't Expire

We live in an economic system that is skills-based, but what exactly does that mean or should it mean?

Many of us might automatically think about the skills that one gains from formalized training or education, but what about those skills that aren't taught? The ones that some of us might have learned as a result of some good old-fashioned home training or experiential knowledge.

Whether I am preparing to partner with someone, contract with a freelancer, or engage in a team-oriented project, I have found that these five skills are cornerstones for success.

Timeliness

Think about time as a precious, natural resource. Most projects and consumerable goods are time-sensitive. Deadlines are often determined by the client or in conjunction with the client. An ability to meet or even exceed those stated deadlines can add tremendous and measurable value to your tenure as an entrepreneur.

Yes, life will happen and when it does, be sure to keep your clients informed if you are going to miss a deadline or if you need an extension. Typically, the work that we do has other moving parts and when we miss deadlines, it may have implications for the rest of the project.

By giving clients notice, you better equip them to make the necessary accommodations on their end.

Problem Solving

Although there are many great resources—print and digital—available to us about freelancing, entrepreneurship, and our fields and industries, there are certain things that entrepreneurs have to figure out simply by doing them. This often requires activating one's problem-solving or critical thinking skills.

Because we can't always anticipate what's to come, the best way to fine-tune your problem-solving skills is to think through "what if" scenarios, always keeping in mind the end goals and the desired outcomes. If you have grown accustomed to doing things a particular way, think about workarounds or various plan B's.

Effective Communication

The ability to effectively communicate is becoming increasingly more important in a culture that relies extensively on abbreviations, acronyms, and lingo. As entrepreneurs, the ability to articulate what you do, why it is of value (especially for potential clients), and why your services are needed can make the difference between your closing a deal and missing out on one. The keys are being able to write and speak well.

If public speaking is not something that you enjoy doing, you may want to look into local organizations that offer public speaking workshops or you may even consider taking a public speaking course at your local community college or hiring a coach.

The same is true for writing. It doesn't matter if you write an email a day or a blog post a week, the ability to write well is a commodifiable skill that can aid any freelancer. As with anything, time on task will help you gain stamina, confidence, and a stronger command of the language.

Working Well Independently and With Others
Co-working, group projects, and cohorts have become major trends in corporate America and at many colleges and universities. Understandably, it is important that people can work together in multiple settings with diverse groups. Yet, it's equally true that in order for any team to operate, all of its members must be able to work well, not just when working together, but independently as well.

Teamwork does make the dream work and there is no "I" in team. However, if no one is looking over your shoulders or holding you accountable, are you just as productive? The key is understanding your intrinsic motivations. Your ability to perform or work well should not be contingent upon external factors. Being a self-starter and being self-driven equips you to work well by yourself or in groups/ teams.

Being Positive
This, by far, is my favorite. I firmly believe that having and maintaining a positive outlook is paramount to being a successful freelancer. Going into projects optimistically and with great care and concern for your clients can lead to a healthy attitude about the work

that you are doing.

This is not to say that you have to be positive about everything all of the time, but it is to say that if you focus on what you can control and you operate under the assumption of goodwill, your good days as a freelancer will far outweigh your bad days.

Yes, Soft Skills Matter
Timeliness, problem solving, effective communication, an ability to work well independently and with others and being positive are five skills that some people may refer to as soft skills. But these soft skills are probably equally as important, if not more important, than some of the other skills that are needed to advance in one's field. Regardless of your industry, focusing on and fine-tuning these can lead to great long-term success for entrepreneurs.

Is your Net Worth your Network?

I am not very good at networking, but as we grow, I realize that it is a key to sustainability. In fact, if given the choice between attending a networking event and sitting at home reading a book, give me the book.

The reality is that networking is not always the most comfortable space for some people. Having to interact, mingle, and make small talk while also marketing your services or explaining what you do can be difficult. Yet it is almost impossible to be a successful freelancer or entrepreneur if you don't take the time to figure out who you want to network with and why.

Start where you are
How many other entrepreneurs do you know? Do they know that you freelance as well? I'll be honest that it wasn't until I started freelancing that I realized that I had peers who had been doing it for years. These people became my most immediate network; I could draw from their experiences and ask them for advice.

They helped me navigate the freelancing landscape and often served as great resources when I was looking for projects and learning how to maximize project boards while building up my clientele.

Be clear about what you want/need from people
I have been accused of being anti-social or aloof in social settings. In part, it is because small talk just does not work for me and my personality type. Talking about what someone watched on TV last night and how many Pampers the average 4-month-old goes through is torturous. I prefer meaningful and transparent conversations that help me to clearly understand the connection, if any, that I have with someone.

Of course, the exchange of pleasantries is necessary before one can make a connection, but it is important to be aware that you are networking for professional purposes and not taking applications for a new best friend.

This makes the process much less exhausting, much more rewarding, and definitely more authentic.

Cross-pollinate with other entrepreneurs
I write, but I have found that entrepreneurs in other fields are great resources and they often provide referrals. Think about some of the projects that you have worked on and some of the needs that your clients had that you could not fulfill. As someone who helps aspiring authors, I often need graphic designers as my clients begin to think about book covers and PR materials. I make sure that I keep several highly skilled freelance graphic designers in my mental Rolodex so that I can send clients their way. In turn, they often refer authors to me.

Because we have mutually benefited from the relationship, we continue to outsource projects to each other.

Use social media
I have discussed this in great detail previously in this book, but it is worth reiterating here. Before I took a deep dive into working for myself, my social media presence was perfunctory at best. I had 400 friends comprised of people who I knew by name and I could tell you explicitly how we were connected. I may have logged on once or twice a week just to say "hi".

As much as I did not like social media, I was missing out on opportunities to network with people who had similar experiences and professional aspirations. I made a conscious decision to be more present and to actively seek out groups and pages for writers, editors, and entrepreneurs in general.

In the process, I discovered that networking was actually easier for me online than in traditional settings. I even set up a page for my company which has led to numerous leads and several contracts.

When it comes to freelancing, there has to be some level of intentionality. I have found that "if you build it, they will come" doesn't apply here. You have to build it and let people know that it's built. For me, networking was a critical part of that process.

You Don't Have to Give Up Your Lifestyle to Be Free

As I type this, my three-month-old nephew sits in his play chair looking up and smiling, with a toothless grin, at the lights. He's too young to understand what I am doing, but there is something endearing about the fact that he can, indirectly, be a part of this freelancing journey with me. In fact, the ability to work from home and to spend quality time with family is a motivating force for many of us who freelance.

An even stronger force is the ability to support and provide for oneself and one's family. Yet, many people may pause before becoming full-time entrepreneurs because of the fear that they will not be able to sustain a livable wage or they will have to give up their quality of life in order to make freelancing work for them. This fear, in turn, may dissuade some people from leaving the traditional 9 to 5 trajectory. It is an honest reaction that I am sure many of us have probably experienced at some point on this journey.

Furthering this trepidation to freelance, some of the popular job sites and job boards offer pay that is, unfortunately, unfair. As recently as May of 2019, I saw a freelancing writing gig that amounted to $1.00 a page. Assuming that it takes someone 5 minutes to write a page of content, that equates to $12.00 an hour. Bidding on contracts is another popular way for entrepreneurs to gain employment and contracts; I recently saw a post where someone's bid on a writing project was less than the national minimum wage.

Perhaps these are some of the horror stories that you have heard or experienced yourself. Both of these examples would probably deter most people from seeing freelancing as more than just a side gig or secondary source of income. With some industries offering such poor compensation, it may also seem as if it is impossible to become a full-time independent worker and make a decent living.

But, as I have discovered, these snapshots do not tell the entire story. Actually, recent statistics suggest that the American workforce is not only changing, but so is the way that workers are being compensated. Not only are more Americans becoming self-employed, but many are thriving financially.

A recent *Forbes* article written by Elaine Pofeldt, author of *The Million Dollar, One Person Business*, suggests that the average freelancer makes more than the average American worker. Pofeldt writes that:

> "The average income for full-time independent workers in 2018 was $69,100, just slightly higher than 2017 ($68,100). For comparison, the median family household income in the U.S. was $59,039 in 2016, the most recent year for which data was available."
>
> https://www.forbes.com/sites/elainepofeldt/2018/07/12/new-data-six-figure-freelancing-is-on-the-rise/#2c9eb11f2a94

As reflected by these numbers, being an independent—creative or otherwise—does not necessarily mean that one has to go without life's comforts. Conversely, I suspect that the ability to maintain what we have become accustomed to calling a 'middle class' lifestyle has led to an uptick in the number of people who freelance full-time.

It is important to note that certain industries are more inclined to pay higher wages. Specifically, full-time independents in the tech and pharmaceutical industries tend to earn more than their peers. Yet, even with some entrepreneurs commanding more than others, which is logical in a free enterprise society, the overall news is still encouraging.

The MBO Partners State of Independence in America 2018 reports that:

> "Companies are growing more comfortable working with independents, utilizing their skills in strategic positions, and paying them more. As a result, the number of High-Earning Independents, those earning more than 100,000, continues to rise—to 3.3 million…Independents remain a powerful economic force, contributing more than $1.3 trillion annually to the economy, more than 6.7% of the U.S. GDP."
> https://www.mbopartners.com/state-of-independence

Although numbers don't always tell the entire story—there is so much more to happiness than material comfort—they do help to eradicate the idea that freelancing leads to a hand-to-mouth lifestyle. With more and more people considering freelancing as a way of life, these statistics are also encouraging because empirical data is often more persuasive than anecdotal evidence about the values and benefits of freelancing.

Sustainability Means Never Stop Learning

I am going back to school. Well, not really, at least not in a conventional sense. I am, however, signed up to take a few courses that should not only enhance my business skills, but also provide me with an opportunity to better understand best practices, new trends, and the ever-changing world of entrepreneurship.

It all started a few weeks ago when we celebrated my mom's 80th birthday. As we wrapped up a weeklong celebration, we talked about her desires and fears about being an octogenarian. Almost every aspect of our conversation revolved around the importance of being a life-long learner. She even challenged me to go back to school.

At first, I dismissed her—I am schooled out. But shortly thereafter, I talked to a client, who is also an octogenarian, and what did our conversation revolve around? You guessed it—lifelong learning.

Seeing this as an *Alchemis*t-like sign, I figured that I shouldn't ignore it. So, I did a simple Google search and after sifting through a spectrum of course offerings ranging from questionable online schools to reputable MBA programs with rigid prerequisites, I came across a jewel in the form of edX: https://www.edx.org/
Founded in 2012, edX has been around for over 5 years. It is a MOOC or massive open online course provider. The courses are marketed as being university level and they range in duration. Partnering with schools like UC Berkeley and Georgetown, edX offers a range of courses that one can select from.

Many of the courses are free if you opt to audit them. If you prefer to go the certification route, the prices seem reasonable, especially if you consider this expenditure as a worthwhile investment in yourself.

Topics range from writing and program management courses to doing business with emergent markets. There is even a section specifically for Business and Management: https://www.edx.org/course?subject=Business%20%26%20Management. I found the courses to be intriguing and to be honest, overwhelming at first.

With over 444 courses in the Business and Management section alone, it may be time consuming sorting through them all. Thankfully, the site is user friendly and you can refine your search based upon criteria such as availability, subject matter, level and even language. Although some of the courses are set for certain time frames (e.g. May 2019), there are still plenty of courses available for this fall, winter and even some for next spring.

Additionally, it is worth noting that many of the courses are self-paced and they are taught by university professors. The self-paced model used for most of the edX courses makes it ideal for the freelancer who is short on time, but who still has a sincere desire to learn more about his/her craft or the industry.

For example, a course titled "Entrepreneurial Operations: Launch a Startup" is taught by an Assistant Professor from Babson University. The course is described as follows:

> This startup operations course will examine the real-world

operational challenges and execution risks associated with getting a new venture started. We will consider start-up ventures in a variety of industries. The course will provide you with a set of steps, frameworks, and tools that can be used to understand the important considerations for building a startup operation from scratch.

In each module, the students will be exposed to a different operations-related concept. Lecture notes, readings, and case studies will explore the key operations topics that are important for start-ups. To learn more about the course or to sign up: https://www.edx.org/course/operations-for-entrepreneurs

As someone who never attended business school and who learned about the business side of freelancing AFTER I started freelancing, this course sounds like it would be worthwhile.

And perhaps what is most beneficial about the edX course offerings is that the courses are diverse enough that they should appeal to a range of entrepreneurs from neophytes to 30-year veterans. With no prerequisites, no GRE or GMAT, the courses truly are accessible; there is even an app so that you can take your classes on the go. This seems perfect for those of us who hope to absorb as much as we can in pursuit of entrepreneurial success.

I have registered for two courses; one starts in November and the other is self-paced. Hopefully, you will find a course that you like. If not right now then consider bookmarking an edX class for the future.

Don't Overlook These Minor Details When Scaling Up Your Business

Bigger is better or is it? Many of us may have aspirational goals of growing our enterprises or scaling up. Who doesn't want more clients? More projects? More revenue? Not casting a universal net, but it is probably fair to say that even if becoming a Fortune 50 company is not your heart's desire, longevity is and longevity often requires scaling up your business.

What does it mean to scale up?
The concept of scaling or scaling up is actually derived from the math concept of making "something larger in size, amount, etc. than it used to be." Something as simple as going from 5 clients to 7 clients can be considered scaling up. Or even growing from 2 employees to 4 requires a change. Even though these numbers may seem small, or inconsequential, any time we add to what we do, it changes the dynamic of what we do.

As much as the idea of scaling up is appealing, to be successful at it, you need to be prepared. Here are 3 details that are easy to overlook, but you may want to consider them as you prepare for the future.

Detail 1: Having more responsibilities, including people to oversee, requires you to understand how you lead.
I admit that I love the art and technical side of writing more than I love the commerce side. For many of us, scaling up often includes bringing on extra help. For some, this is a relatively seamless transition. For others, having to take on the added task of supervising or overseeing other people may not come naturally.

To help prepare, try to determine your leadership or managerial style. Leadership styles can range from being an autocratic leader to engaging in more of a hands-on, participant style of leadership https://smallbusiness.chron.com/5-different-types-leadership-styles-17584.html.

Because I have a tendency to focus on motivating and inspiring those around me, I consider myself a transformative leader. Before I scaled up, I sat down and I thought about the deficiencies with this type of leadership style, specifically, I have a tendency to give people 3rd, 4th, and 5th chances after they mess up. This may be great for some industries, but I knew that it would cause problems as my company grew.

So, I surrounded myself with people who were more detail oriented and results-driven. I can focus on the bigger picture and they make sure that we have met or exceeded our clients' expectations. They're managerial style is transactional which is "a straightforward leadership style with a focus on work, reward and processes that drive consistent results."

Knowing that this was not my strong point better equipped me to identify what I needed others around me to do. The more that you understand how you lead *before you grow*, the more you will be able to take on this new role without feeling as if you are being compartmentalized or being forced to do something that makes you feel uncomfortable or compromised.

Detail 2: As you grow, so does your liability and your overhead. Scaling up is not just about having employees. It is also about the addition of new products and services that affect your bottom line and can lead to greater costs. For example, I did not initially take credit cards because most of my clients paid by other means. As I scaled up, I decided to start adding new services such as book cover designs and press releases.

Perhaps it was a coincidence, but around the same time that I added these new services, potential clients started asking about credit card payments. Now, credit card sales account for 60% of our payment methods which means that I now have to factor in processing fees as a part of my overhead. Sure 2.9% to 3.1% may not seem like a lot, but for large ticket items, it can add up.

Another minor detail that often gets overlooked is insurance. Make sure you increase your insurance coverage and protect your assets. Being a solo entrepreneur has many advantages, but there are also limitations as it relates to your ability to grow and expand. As such, your insurance needs will often grow and expand as your business does.

Before you scale up, make sure you understand how it will affect your liability. Consult with a licensed insurance broker who can make sure that your coverage is aligned to your needs. He/she will be able to help you understand if your current policy, such as umbrella insurance, is the best option for a business of your size.

Like anything attached to progress, growing pains may be inevitable. By being proactive before you scale up, you can identify the required puzzle pieces before you start putting it together.

Reboot as Needed

As I bring *Time to Pivot* to its close, I want to share with you a valuable lesson that I have learned from every successful person who I have personally worked with or who has been one of our clients: Be willing to reinvent yourself.

Companies and businesses that do not reinvent themselves to meet market demands tend to go out of business. Did you ever imagine that Toys R Us would not be around for future generations?

For most of us the answer to that question is 'no'. Unfortunately Toys R Us waited too late to capitalize on a digital format. By the time that they realized that brand loyalty alone would not sustain them, it was too late to regain the customers who left them for online retailers—some of whom were able to offer the same products for a lower cost. In other words, they waited too late to pivot.

Throughout this book, I have offered stories, anecdotes, illustrations and real-world examples to help illuminate why pivoting is one of the single most important factors in a business idea becoming a successful reality.

As with anything that is nuanced, there is not a specific age or gestation period before it is time to make a move—much of this will depend on where you are in life and the developmental stage of your business. I do want to state that regardless of where you are, it is not where you will always be.

In fact, as you reflect back to your ideation stage, think about all of the progress that you have made. Too many of us allow fear to consume us and we don't move at all. Now, think about how you are currently executing your idea. Lastly, reflect on what sustainability looks like for you.

It's important that you celebrate your movement not just from the vantage point of your immediate goals, but also from the standpoint of your long-term goals. By doing this, it will keep you from becoming too myopic. I highly recommend that you periodically review your systems, processes, and infrastructures.

In fact, when is the last time that you got in the proverbial weeds and carefully examined your businesses practices? Is it time for a shift? Is it time to reboot? Are you growing? Have you gotten too comfortable?

These are difficult, yet necessary, questions to ask and answer. Most companies, even Fortune 100, reboot as needed. Fresh leadership, new innovations, advanced technology or even a changing demographic can push us to think about what we are doing well and what we need to do differently.

Just as your computer system occasionally needs an update and you need to reboot it to get the most up-to-date improvements, your business deserves the same.

As I mentioned in one of the opening chapters, for many of us, our best lessons are born out of mistakes, failures, or things that did not go as planned. Rather than seeing these failures as personal flaws or reflections of one's ability, see them as opportunities to get better. In other words, acknowledge your failures and then leverage them to improve.

Take the time to ask: How is your business doing? What have these last years taught you about yourself? Where are your gaps? What areas need to be improved upon? How do you plan to move forward and embrace these changes?

Once you have identified areas that didn't go so well, step back and assess whether or not the failure was within your control. Was it preventable and is it correctable moving into 2019? Identifying the cause of failure with great certainty may be difficult to do, especially if there are other people involved. It's much easier to shift blame to a team member, a peer, or someone/something else.

Honestly, it is not easy to acknowledge our role in goof-ups/mistakes/failures, but we must. It is only by holding up a mirror and paying careful attention to what reflects back at us that we can grow and improve.

Before you can glean the lesson from the failure, you first have to acknowledge the failure and make sure that it was, indeed, a failure. Sometimes we are too difficult on ourselves or our expectations are unrealistic. For example, if your goal was to acquire 100 new clients in 2019 and you only obtained 75, is that really a failure or was your original goal too unrealistic for your market?

Looking at this through a reflective lens, one may discover that the original goal should have been 75 new clients based on the previous years' successes, demand for the service, and one's geographic location. The lesson isn't that you failed by not obtaining those last 25 clients, but that your metrics need to be retooled when mapping out your goals.

Like Coach Furcron, my father had this thing about defeatist talk. Certain words, especially "can't," were forbidden in our household while I was growing up. This forced us to problem solve, engage in conflict resolution, address our difficulties and define our problems without feeling powerless and hopeless. This also taught us how to accept life's punches without getting knocked out.

Ostensibly, I am not a fan of dwelling on one's mistakes for too long. As soon as you have a grasp on what didn't go well and why, it's time to move on. Unfortunately, I have seen entrepreneurs who have had bad years and who have wanted to throw in the towel, but, often, this was because they focused too much on the emotions that failure evokes and they didn't think in terms of how to turn things around.

My point: Don't give too much energy to what went wrong; instead, put new effort towards repurposing your goals or creating new ones. To continue sustaining your company with great confidence and poise, map out your goals. In fact, write them down using action verbs. Instead of writing down, 'make more money' write down 'generate 5 new contracts valued at $3,000 each.'

The key is planning and executing with clear, measurable benchmarks sprinkled along the way. Remember that all goals should be clearly articulated, specific, and realistic. By being focused and intentional, you can realistically sustain your business for many, many years to come.

Thank you for taking this journey with me. Remember, ask yourself—is it time to pivot?

ABOUT THE AUTHOR

A native of Detroit, Michigan, Dr. Tyra Seldon earned her Ph.D. in English literature and language from the University of Rochester. She has served as an English instructor and professor at the University of Rochester (NY), Dickinson College (PA), Anderson University and Martin University (IN). After a successful teaching career in higher education and K-12, she launched Seldon Writing Group, LLC in 2011.

In her role as founder and CEO, Dr. Seldon serves as a writing consultant and content developer for several national initiatives, organizations, and Fortune 500 companies. Clients have included educational companies OpenEd (ACT), Learning Express, and McGraw Hill Education. Dr. Seldon also conducts numerous webinars and workshops for business leaders, school districts, not-for-profits, and community organizations.

Whether it is as an education advocate, public intellectual, writing coach, mentor or small business owner, Dr. Seldon is passionate about using her gifts to help others. Additionally, her articles have appeared in *Slant, Freelancer's Union, Black Coffy, Black Doctor, Shoppe Black* and *Your Black Education*.

Dr. Seldon is available to conduct workshops, speaking engagements, and conduct training sessions. Please contact: staff@seldonwritinggroup.com or contact us at www.seldonwritinggroup.com

www.ingramcontent.com/pod-product-compliance
Lightning Source LLC
Chambersburg PA
CBHW031623210526
45464CB00004B/1727